Citizens and subjects

Citizens and subjects is an essay on the nature and condition of democracy in Britain at the end of the twentieth century. It examines the commonly held view that Britain is a model democracy, and argues that this is a dangerous myth inhibiting both radical thought and serious constitutional change. Exploring the tradition of political and constitutional thought in Britain, the book draws a comparison with contemporary political reality to reveal a wide gulf between the theory and the practice.

Dr Wright considers the problem in its historical context, arguing that Britain suffers from a particularly acute form of a general problem of modern government. While we think of ourselves as a liberal democracy, the fact is that our liberalism was in place long before democracy came onto the agenda. From the outset, democracy was seen as a problem by both conservatives and liberals – and was often misunderstood by socialists.

In recent years democratic and constitutional issues have again emerged as a matter of concern and debate, as with the campaign of Charter 88. Although Dr Wright does discuss the means by which the present closed and centralized system might be converted into a pluralistic, open and participatory democracy, he argues that practical reforms will not be possible unless they are also linked to a new tradition of radical constitutional thought.

Tony Wright was Reader in Political Studies at the University of Birmingham until 1992. He is now a Labour MP.

Citizens and subjects

An essay on British politics

Tony Wright

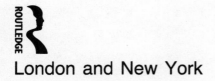

London and New York

First published 1994
by Routledge
11 New Fetter Lane, London EC4P 4EE

Simultaneously published in the USA and Canada
by Routledge
29 West 35th Street, New York, NY 10001

© 1994 Tony Wright

Phototypeset in Bembo by Intype, London

Printed and bound in Great Britain by T.J. Press (Padstow) Ltd,
Padstow, Cornwall

Printed on acid free paper

British Library Cataloguing in Publication Data
A catalogue record for this book is available from the British Library

Library of Congress Cataloging in Publication Data has been applied for

ISBN 0–415–04964–4

Contents

Preface

What follows is what it says it is: an essay, no more and (I hope) no less. It is, though, an essay with an argument, even perhaps a tract. As such, it covers a large territory in short compass and no doubt lingers too briefly at some of the more difficult corners. But I wanted to get it off my chest, and in a form that was of manageable length and friendly in its structure. It will, I hope, be of some interest to both citizens and students (which is not to suggest that these are necessarily incompatible categories).

The argument is that there is an unresolved problem about democracy in Britain and that this is a fundamental fact in understanding (and reforming) our political system – and much else besides. I have sought to explore this from a number of angles and directions and to suggest some possible lines of advance. In my view, mechanical and institutional reform, which is badly needed, will not be achieved or prove successful unless it is rooted in a basis of *ideas* capable of sustaining and nourishing it. That is my central theme and focus here.

Perhaps I should add that the completion of this essay was interrupted by the General Election of April 1992, when I was redeployed from the University of Birmingham to the House of Commons. Subsequent observation of British parliamentary democracy at close quarters has done nothing to diminish my belief that here is a system in urgent need of concerted democratic reform. Quite the reverse.

A.W.W.
1993

1

The image and the system

An observer who looks at the living reality will wonder at the contrast to the paper description.

Walter Bagehot *The English Constitution* (1867)

Everybody knows that Britain is a democracy. Our leaders regularly tell us so. They are supported, with only minor qualification, by the great constitutional authorities of the recent past and the textbook writers of the recent present. Indeed, when the blood really starts pumping, we are liable to be told that we are not merely a democracy, but the quintessential democracy, the mother and father of all democracies, the veritable *fons et origa* of the democratic principle itself and the pre-eminent exponent of its living reality.

The blood was clearly pumping for erstwhile Prime Minister Margaret Thatcher at the Rome summit of the European Community in October 1990. Isolated at the summit, she lashed out at her fellow European leaders at the post-summit press conference. Only she (she declared) would be returning to a political system which required her not only to make a statement in the House of Commons on the summit, but then to be questioned extensively on it. It was a claim to democratic superiority. Nor was this the end of the story. In the ensuing Commons exchanges (as a result of which she managed to lose her Deputy Prime Minister and provoke a major crisis for her party and a terminal one for her leadership – a rueful postscript to her earlier remarks), she denounced the threat to British democracy posed by the institutions of the European Community. Would she give up the sovereignty of the British Parliament? The answer was 'No, No, No'.[1]

It was, perhaps, inevitable that this episode should have been regarded primarily as a political crisis rather than as a moment for political and constitutional reflection. Such reflection has not been a marked characteristic of the recent British political tradition. Traditional constitutional reflexes could still be called upon, just, whether in the invocation of parliamentary 'sovereignty' by politicians or the tabloid exhortation to raise a chant of 'Up Yours, Delors' in the general direction of the President of the European Commission. Yet these reflexes seemed remembered and mechanical, rather than vital and active, evoking a response that was at best sluggish and ambiguous. Something had clearly changed – but what?

There was manifestly a problem about sovereignty. The gap between the constitutional theory and the political and economic reality had become so wide and visible that the old rhetoric could no longer bridge it. Sovereignty was abridged every day and in every way. Blackstone's old doctrine about Parliament being able to do anything that was not naturally impossible omitted to mention the Bundesbank. Even in formal constitutional terms, the combined effects of the Treaty of Rome and the Single European Act (even without the addition of the Maastricht Treaty) meant that it was no longer possible just to go on telling the old story in the old way. The real problem with the rhetoric of sovereignty was that it actually obscured the substance of power. Intended as a claim about its unique source, its effect was to blur the real nature of its exercise.

Earlier in the century, in the context of another kind of debate about sovereignty, the political theorist Harold Laski declared that 'the sovereign state of philosophic theory never existed except in the imagination of philosophers'.[2] If we were to find the basis for a democratic pluralism, then it was necessary to drop the fiction of sovereignty and get to grips with the realities of power:

> It would be of lasting benefit to political science if the whole concept of sovereignty were surrendered. That, in fact, with which we are dealing is power; and what is important in the nature of power is the end it seeks to serve and the way in which it serves that end.[3]

This observation is as relevant to the argument about the 'sovereignty' of the British state in relation to other states as it is to the internal organization of the British state itself. Power can be shared; sovereignty, strictly, cannot. The former opens up possibilities for new organizational forms; the latter blocks them off. Yet we are surely in need of such new forms, both internationally and domestically, if the exercise of power on a range of fronts and in relation to a range of issues is to be effective and democratic. Nor are these two concepts unrelated. A major ingredient of effectiveness is legitimacy; and the language of sovereignty no longer fills the cracks that have conspicuously opened up in the legitimating cement of Britain's governing arrangements.

Indeed, what is striking about the 'sovereignty of Parliament' argument as it has been deployed in recent British politics is that its role has been to block a whole range of proposals and developments – from closer European integration to the enhanced protection of individual rights – on the grounds that they are in conflict with the doctrine. It is a blocking doctrine, not an enabling one. It is the doctrine to be summoned up to explain why things cannot be done: why the courts cannot challenge the constitutionality of legislation, 'why there cannot be a guarantee of basic rights, why government in Britain cannot be federalized, why local government can have no constitutional status, why new forms of representation and accountability and redress are not possible. The point, for the moment, is not that these are all necessarily desirable developments (though I think they are), but that the debate about their desirability simply hits the ring-fence of a doctrine which prevents arguments getting any further. It is the no-doctrine of British politics.

It is also, like the concept of sovereignty itself, a fiction. It conceals the exercise of power rather than identifying and illuminating it. British government takes the form of parliamentary sovereignty (more precisely, of the Crown-in-Parliament), but the substance of something very different. When Mrs Thatcher heralded her return from that European summit to the questioning of the House of Commons as evidence of the democratic vitality of a sovereign Parliament, this represented the triumph of form over substance. She also returned to a country where there was more unease about the democratic credentials of government than at any period in recent history. Certainly, governments were voted in and there were regular opportunities to boot them out. The ability to 'kick the rascals out' is the bottom line of democracy, and fortunate are those peoples, like the British, in secure possession of that ability. But democracy is not just about the bottom line. Modern government is big government. The growth of big government has outstripped the ability of representative institutions to keep up. As Poggi puts it, the fact that the modern state still functions through forms inherited from the last century means that assemblies lack effectiveness and are 'reduced to a highly visible stage on which are enacted vocal, ritualized confrontations between preformed, hierarchically controlled, ideologically characterized alignments'.[4]

This is a general problem of modern government. It is the problem of the democratic government of twentieth (and, soon, twenty-first) century societies on the basis of political institutions developed in and for an earlier and different kind of society. It is the problem of democracy arriving as a 'top dressing' (in C. B. Macpherson's phrase)[5] on existing liberal states, a reminder that behind the comfortable coupling of 'liberal democracy' is the fact of the liberalism being in place before the democracy. There is, then, a problem of democracy in all modern states, notwithstanding their possession of the visible and vital badges of democratic government (such as free elections and oppositions). Peter Self makes the essential point:

> It is necessary for democratic institutions to adapt their workings so as to meet the necessities of modern governmental agendas. Should this fail to occur, democracies may fail to sustain acceptable standards of executive performance, or alternatively power will seep away to hidden bureaucracies, or to some type of 'business government', leaving political institutions increasingly formalistic.[6]

He might have added that there are evident dangers in democracy coming to be seen as a matter of form rather than of substance.

It is all the more necessary to identify this as a general problem, across societies and political systems, precisely because the argument here is that – for a whole range of reasons yet to be discussed – Britain experiences the problem in a particularly acute form and, in consequence, suffers from some of its most troublesome effects. The further argument is that the task of giving a contemporary meaning to the democratic idea, a meaning capable of articulation in a public philosophy and incorporation in a range of institutions and practices, has become an urgent one. Indeed, from a number of directions it is being actively attempted, and democratic theory is positively flourishing.[7] But so is anti-democratic theory, anxious to protect and insulate the policy process from the impact of democratic politics. Nor is it surprising that there should be wide disagreement about the meaning and content of the axial legitimating ideology of modern political life. This has always been, and remains, massively contested. A survey for UNESCO in 1949, with questionnaires completed by scholars in many countries, yielded the following unsurprising conclusions:

i   There were no replies averse to democracy. Probably for the first time in history, 'democracy' is claimed as the proper ideal description of all systems of political and social organization advocated by influential proponents.

ii The idea of democracy was considered ambiguous and even those who thought that it was clear or capable of clarity were obliged to admit a certain ambiguity either in the institutions or devices employed to effect the idea or in the cultural or historical circumstances by which word, idea, and practice are conditioned.[8]

I do not pretend that such ambiguities are easily removed. Indeed, they are intrinsic to the idea of democracy. It is only necessary to recall the standing disagreement between those for whom democracy is an argument about a kind of society and those for whom it is a description of a kind of political system. Or between those for whom it is a protective device against those with power and those for whom it is a claim to the active exercise of power. These matters are not pursued here, although they necessarily arise along the way. Democracy is an argument about the exercise of power and a claim to citizenship. The arguments and the claim relate crucially to the political system, but they also relate to other arenas of power and citizenship in society. I am interested here in looking at how some of these issues have been discussed in Britain. My conclusion is that they have been discussed in such a way that leaves democracy peculiarly undeveloped. When it should be as complex and multi-dimensional as the structure of power with which it is now faced, its status is that of a comfortable achievement of the past rather than an urgent challenge for the present.

Indeed, it is scarcely too much to say, adapting Bagehot, that democracy has become part – a crucial part – of the 'dignified' ideology of British politics. I want to advance the heresy that the British political tradition has never taken democracy very seriously. I want to suggest that there are cultural, constitutional and ideological reasons for this. The effects of not taking it seriously have become apparent for all to see. When Mrs Thatcher returned from that European summit, having handbagged those European politicians with the British version of democracy, it was to a House of Commons which had recently come closer to defeating the Government than it had in over a decade. The great issue it chose was the control of dogs; but even then it could not quite manage to bite as well as bark.

When the decisive bite did come, a few weeks later, and Mrs Thatcher fell, what was significant and revealing was that this was not the action of a sovereign Parliament, let alone of a sovereign people, but of an internal party putsch. Equally, the travails of her successor are rooted in the *internal* fault lines of his party. Parliamentary sovereignty provides a cloak of legitimacy for executive and party dominance. It permits British governments, with only a minority of electoral support, to claim a bogus majoritarianism. It produces a system which is allegedly strong, but which is notoriously weak in terms of such democratic criteria as representation, accountability, participation and openness.

This helps to unravel one of the central paradoxes of modern British government. It might seem odd that a political system and political tradition in which strong, uninhibited executive action has enjoyed such a primacy has also been distinguished by a history of policy failures and discontinuities on so many fronts, an inability to construct durable institutions within the policy process and – of course – the economic and social consequences of such failure. Yet it is precisely because of the democratic weaknesses that the executive strength has in this sense proved so illusory. It has lacked the foundations on which to build. This is just one of the peculiarities of the British to which we shall have to return.

There is, then, plainly a gap between the traditional ideology of British politics – even its continued recitation by the politicians sounds increasingly hollow – and contemporary reality. The recognition of this gap, and of its baneful consequences, has sharpened appreciably in recent years, from a variety of directions and reflecting an assortment of approaches and remedies. At the beginning of this century the American A. L. Lowell observed that: 'The typical Englishman believes that his government is incomparably the best in the world. It is the thing above all others that he is proud of.'[9] In mid–century the Frenchman André Mathiot was equally celebratory: the British political system stood as an 'enviable model of democratic government'.[10] In the 1960s, political scientists constructed landmark interpretations of British politics which emphasised its neatly balanced theoretical under-pinnings as the clue to the consensual stability of its system of 'representative and responsible government'.[11] In the past two decades all that has changed. The old interpretations no longer carry conviction, but there are not yet new ones to take their place. There is a crisis of both theory and practice in British government. I want to argue that, in significant measure, this is to be seen as the consequence of a political tradition in which democracy has not been taken very seriously; and that this deficiency will have to be attended to in any reconstruction of the theory and practice of British politics. But for fear of frightening the horses, it would not be too much to say that Britain needs a democratic revolution.

2

The place and the problem

No one . . . can doubt that by 1900 . . . the English consti-
tution had been transformed into something like a democracy.
A. V. Dicey *Lectures on the Relation between Law and Public
Opinion during the Nineteenth Century* (1905)

It may seem absurd to suggest that democracy has not been taken
seriously in Britain when it – or 'something like' it in Dicey's
phrase – could plausibly be said to have been in place since the
beginning of the century. Plausibly, but misleadingly. It is not
just a matter of quibbles, though scarcely trivial ones, to the effect
that in 1900 full manhood suffrage had yet to be achieved, that
women were entirely excluded from the suffrage and would not
be included on parity with men for another quarter century, that
such supports of democratic politics as payment of elected members were still absent, that forms of plural voting remained until
mid-century, and that the House of Lords – as the budget crisis
of 1909–11 was to show – remained a major undemocratic player
in British politics. Against the self-image, it is worth recording
that pre–1914 Britain had the most restricted franchise of any
'democratic' state except Hungary.[1]

However, such facts are the least significant part of the story.
What matters is the context within which they are set. Here the
record is of a political tradition of a distinctive kind, in which the
arrival of democratic ideas posed particular problems and issued
in particular conclusions. It is only necessary to recall the anxious
and anguished debates surrounding the suffrage extensions of the
nineteenth century to see something of what is involved. If democracy was about the arrival of the masses in politics, it scared the
life out of the classes. It made conservatives want to resist and

liberals want to worry. It represented the spectre of the untutored poor finding the means to expropriate property and destroy culture, liberty and civilization. At the very least, therefore, it was to be seen (as it was, for example, by both Disraeli and Bagehot) as a problem of political management or (as it was by John Stuart Mill) as a school for moral improvement.

In other words, democracy entered British political culture as a problem and remained so until at least the beginning of this century. The First World War of 1914–18 can now be seen to have been crucial in effecting a change in its status. A modern war, involving a whole population, needed a modern and popular ideology; and that is what democracy supplied. To quote the title of a 1917 pamphlet by R. H. Tawney, the war was about *Democracy or Defeat*.[2] At one level, then, democracy had become a good thing, a cause worth fighting for, the basis for a modern ideological self-image. This was a development of considerable significance. At another level, though, the doubts and difficulties remained, suggesting that the matter of democracy had not lost its problematic status in Britain.

It was clear, for example, that the old nineteenth-century fears about the consequences of the arrival of the working class – the 'masses' – into organized political life were still not far beneath the surface, despite the formal embrace of the ideology of democracy. Such fears may be glimpsed in Ramsay Muir's account of *How Britain is Governed* (1930), notwithstanding (or perhaps because of) his own impeccable Liberal credentials:

> Look at the faces of any crowd pouring out of a morning train on the way to work – some stupid, some harassed, some predatory, some vacuous, some trivial – and reflect that with them rests the determination of our destiny: however ardent a democrat you may be, you will have some moments of misgiving.[3]

This tells us something about the status of democracy in the British political culture, but there is much more to the story. In particular, there is the question of what Tawney meant in 1917 when he urged a war for 'democracy' – and the extent to which this meaning was accepted or rejected.

What Tawney demanded was that democracy should be regarded as a kind of society, not merely as a political mechanism. Its root was an ethic of equality; its expression was the political, social and economic organization of that egalitarian ethic. That was the cry raised and the promise made ('homes fit for heroes') in 1918, only to be forgotten and transmuted thereafter. It was raised again, with more conviction and power, in the Second World War ('fair shares for all') and underpinned the post-war settlement of the 1940s, which in turn sustained the politics of an entire generation, before the frontal assault of the Thatcher years. It is in this sense that A. J. P. Taylor once remarked that Britain had become a genuine social democracy in 1940 and ceased to be so afterwards. It is in this sense, too, that the 'settlement' of the 1940s may be seen as a definition and settlement of the rights of citizenship – in T. H. Marshall's terms, as a cumulative package of political, social and economic rights[4] – and of democracy itself.

But this is only one democratic tradition. If it flowered briefly but intensely in the 1940s, its roots remained exceptionally shallow and undeveloped. It is not just that the settlement became so easily unsettled, but that so little was actually built upon it. Consider, for example, the protracted failure to develop a quality system of common schooling appropriate to such a democracy. Consider too the consequences of that failure. Or consider the Bullock Report (1977) on industrial democracy, which presented its proposals in terms of a 'magnificent journey' to extend democracy from the political rights established in the 1832 Reform Act to a modern conception of social, economic and industrial citizenship, but which found too few passengers willing to take the trip.[5] I want to suggest later that both the political left and the political right in Britain have had problems with democracy, for different reasons, reinforcing its neglect and preventing it becoming the active constituent of British political culture. But this is not just a matter of the disputed relationship between 'social' and 'political' democracy. Rather, it is a matter of the historic difficulties associated with both.

On one side, there were all the difficulties implied by the arrival of democracy in a society with an elaborately hierarchical social structure and a rigid class system, and with its familiar lubricants of deference and *noblesse oblige*. If democracy was to be seen as a kind of society with a distinctive quality of social relationships – and this was precisely how de Tocqueville had famously characterized it in his *Democracy in America* – then in nineteenth-century Britain this prospect could be viewed as implying nothing less than a social revolution. It is not surprising, therefore, that much

effort was devoted to disarming and domesticating the new democratic ideology, stripping it of dangerous social pretensions and
making it a matter of political mechanisms and political management. Indeed, there were those who found in the nature of the
British social structure and its texture of class relationships precisely the means whereby democracy could be contained and made
safe.

In other words, not merely was there a rejection of the idea of
'social' democracy, but 'political' democracy was to be so
managed that a traditional class structure could be called in aid to
soften its impact. That was the prospect offered by Disraeli's
discovery of the Tory working man – that 'angel in marble' to
be sculpted out of an enlarged electorate.[6] Certainly, the combination of political democracy with the survival of a society distinguished by marked social separation and what Orwell called 'that
accursed itch of class-difference, like the pea under the princess's
mattress'[7] has been a remarkable political achievement, as has the
ability of the Conservative Party to preside over so much of it. It
is equally remarkable that, even in the last decade of the twentieth
century, the failure of social democracy in Britain can still define
its politics. Thus John Major's first prime ministerial prospectus
ran up the flag of 'classlessness' and 'opportunity', a reflection
more of historic failures (or successes) than of imminent achieve-
ments. It was unkindly pointed out that his first cabinet (in 1990,
not 1890) contained not a single woman, that nineteen of its
twenty-one members were the products of public schools, and
that one of his first prime ministerial acts was to bestow a hereditary baronetcy (male line only) on the husband of his predecessor.

Part of the story, then, is of the way in which in Britain the
larger ambitions of democracy, in terms of social equality, were
deliberately and successfully constrained. Democracy was a matter
of certain political arrangements. However – and this is the other
part of the story – in Britain even 'political' democracy raised
particular difficulties and had to be accommodated within an established political and constitutional tradition. It has been well said
that 'in Britain even political democracy had a tough nut to
crack'.[8] It was not the axial principle of the political order, but an
incorporation into a political tradition which, in good Whig terms,
defined its essence as a matter of constitutional mixture and balance with an adaptive capacity to change and develop. The 'Glori-
ous Revolution' was the landmark shift of balance, towards Parlia-

ment and away from Crown, the foundation stone of British liberty and stability. From this perspective, given elegant statement by Burke in the eighteenth century and Macaulay in the nineteenth, the task was to celebrate and defend the 'matchless constitution' against those who did not understand its mysteries and glories and wanted (like the utilitarians and radical democrats) to subject it to drastic surgery.

In Britain, then, there was neither a democratic revolution nor an ideological consensus about democracy. Indeed, the democratic idea and movement encountered an established constitutional doctrine of balance, continuity and adaptation. It encountered further doctrines – like that of 'virtual' representation – which were marshalled against the idea of equal political rights. Even when such resistance was overcome, democracy developed by a process of accommodation and incorporation to an existing constitution (and its doctrines), not as the principle by which that constitution was itself to be reconstructed. Much political discussion centred upon the management of this accommodation, once it was accepted as necessary, and much satisfaction was subsequently taken in the way in which it was accomplished. The 'people' had been admitted to the constitution, but without the need for a new constitutional settlement. Old doctrines and old institutions remained intact. The graft had been successful. Put differently, though, this meant that 'Britain had no real sense of democratic purpose. . . . Democracy might become part of the British political tradition, but it could never define it.'[9]

It is not surprising, therefore, to find that the concept of 'the people' has failed to find a place within the constitution in Britain.[10] The people were an accretion; they did not define its essence. A similar, and allied, distinctiveness of the British political tradition has been the absence of a developed concept of the state, as something requiring organization and arrangement on the basis of defined principles. This was remarked upon in the last century by Matthew Arnold and, in this century, by Ernest Barker and others. There was a governing tradition, but not a state tradition.[11] Foreigners had states; the British had governments. This enabled Dicey to explain why the British should reject any notion of a separate kind of law and courts (like the French *conseil d'état*) to regulate the activities of the state, for in Britain the 'rule of law' knew no such distinctions. Dicey's explanation won widespread assent as the statement of constitutional orthodoxy. It, too, is part of a tradition which has found good reasons for not taking democracy and the state seriously. The absence in Britain of a developed and coherent system of public law appropriate to the needs of a modern democratic state is just one example and consequence of this mode of thinking.

The argument, then, is that in Britain neither qualitative, social democracy nor mechanical, political democracy had an easy ride. The former soon found itself reduced to the latter in most quarters, while political democracy was itself absorbed by existing political and constitutional traditions. This absorption was, eventually, trumpeted as further tribute to the adaptive capacity of the British way of politics, with its unwritten constitution, nicely balanced institutions and supportive political culture. It was not always so clear that the story would come to be written in quite this way. In particular, there was the problem of the relationship between the sovereignty of Parliament, enshrined since 1688 as the foundation principle of the British constitution, and the democratic doctrine of the sovereignty of the people. Even when, and after much dispute, the basis of representation was amended and enlarged so that this particular circle could be squared, there remained the question of what the representatives of the new democracy would do with a sovereign Parliament in an unwritten constitution. There was a certain paradox that a country which prided itself on the historic continuity of its pre-democratic constitution, to which the forces of democracy had to be accommodated, should also have been a country where the opportunities for majoritarian tyranny – so feared by Mill, who had learned it from Tocqueville, and the whole liberal tradition – were potentially so abundant in view of the uncircumscribed nature of parliamentary sovereignty.

As we shall see, such questions have played their part in the recent revival of constitutional argument in Britain; but for a long time, as we shall also see, they did not. By the beginning of this century it was possible to claim (as Dicey did) that the democratic accommodation had been made, that a flexible and informal constitution had successfully effected another historic adjustment. Reluctant conservatives and anxious liberals could discard their darker apprehensions, while socialists could embrace one kind of democracy as the route to another. But it is important to be clear about what had not happened. The arrival of democracy had not been the occasion for a radical reconstruction of the British state, or even for serious inquiry about what the application of demo-cratic ideas to a modern state might involve. Democracy had not entered the bloodstream of British politics. In constitutional terms it remained very much business as usual; but that business could now be conducted in the legitimating language of democratic ideology.

3

Democracy and the constitution: New wine, old bottles

> In England the Parliament has an acknowledged right to modify the constitution; as, therefore, the constitution may undergo perpetual changes, it does not in reality exist.
>
> Alexis de Tocqueville *Democracy in America* Vol. I (1835)

Let us stay with Dicey. For it was almost exactly a century ago that A. V. Dicey, distinguished academic lawyer, produced his *Introduction to the Study of the Law of the Constitution* (1885). This landmark work of constitutional interpretation became the twentieth century orthodoxy, from which generations of students – and even, through the public language of politics, a citizenry – learned an understanding and appreciation of the distinctive characteristics of the British unwritten constitution. What they learned, contrary to Tocqueville, was not that the constitution was a chimera, but that it was firmly rooted in its own secure principles (of parliamentary sovereignty and the rule of law) and customary practices. Borrowing Bryce's distinction between 'rigid' and 'flexible' constitutions, Dicey was able both to describe and celebrate 'the most flexible polity in existence' and to contrast it with 'the rigidity of almost every foreign constitution'.[1]

But was it a democratic constitution? On this key issue Dicey had an important line of argument, and it is worth examining it here. It was necessarily an important argument, since the task was to give an account of the constitution which would carry conviction in the new age of democratic politics. The issue to be negotiated was this: If the sovereignty of Parliament – 'the right to make or unmake any law whatever'[2] – was the foundation principle of the British constitution, how was this to be reconciled with the democratic principle of the sovereign people? Further, what was there to prevent the despotic exercise of sovereign power by a Parliament against a people? Dicey dismissed any notion that the rights of citizens were better protected by formal constitutional declarations 'of the Rights of Man or of Englishmen' than by meeting particular wrongs with particular remedies (thus 'the Habeus Corpus Acts declare no principle and define no rights, but they are for practical purposes worth a hundred constitutional articles guaranteeing individual liberty'),[3] and the terms of that dismissal have also informed twentieth century conventional constitutional wisdom in Britain.

However, his main argument was designed to show not merely that the liberties of Englishmen were secure under the constitution, but that this was because the legal sovereignty of Parliament had to be set within the political sovereignty of the electorate. The theoretical possibility of tyranny was trumped by its practical and political impossibility. Whatever may have been the case in the past, a modern Parliament would never embark upon despotic measures:

> Parliament would not at the present day prolong by law the duration of an existing House of Commons. Parliament would not without great hesitation deprive of their votes large classes of Parliamentary electors; and, speaking generally, Parliament would not embark on a course of reactionary legislation . . . [4]

Legal sovereignty was bounded and conditioned by the realities of political sovereignty. What *could* be done, *would* not be done (which had been Leslie Stephen's point in explaining that Parliament could, but would not, have all blue-eyed babies murdered). There were both external restraints (disobedience and resistance) and internal ones (prudence and respect for opinion). The distinctive merit of a system of representative government was that it ensured a coincidence of these external and internal limitations on the sovereign power.

Thus the aim and effect of representative government was to bring legal sovereignty in line with political sovereignty: 'the essential property of representative government is to produce coincidence between the wishes of the sovereign and the wishes of the subject'.[5] This enables Dicey to claim that, in general terms, 'that which the majority of the House of Commons command, the majority of the English people usually desire'.[6] His further claim, beyond the fact of representative government, was that the

operative customs and conventions of the constitution reflected
and reinforced the political sovereignty of the electorate. These
'understandings' (such as the responsibility of ministers to the
House of Commons) not only ensured the ascendancy of the
elective part of the legislature, but also therefore secured the political ascendancy of the electors themselves. A theoretically supreme
legislature was really the practical expression of a politically
supreme electorate: 'our modern code of constitutional morality
secures, though in a roundabout way, what is called abroad the
"sovereignty of the people".'[7] The way in which the constitution
actually worked brought legal and political sovereignty into har-
mony, on terms which assured the democratic primacy of the
latter. This enabled Dicey to arrive at, and expound, what he
described as 'the fundamental dogma of modern constitutionalism;
the legal sovereignty of Parliament is subordinate to the political
sovereignty of the nation'.[8]

In Dicey's elegant and authoritative hands, the historic and pre-
democratic constitution had been safely navigated without major
structural alteration to a modern democratic interpretation. Its
adaptive, flexible character was vindicated. Its balance had shifted,
but without the need for root-and-branch upheaval of a traditional
institutional landscape. It achieved through its own peculiar practices what less fortunate peoples had been obliged to attempt
through drastic institutional surgery, political insurgency and a
resort to first principles. It was a remarkable story of the way in
which 'the prerogatives of the Crown have become the privileges
of the people'.[9] This last point in the Diceyan interpretation is
worth emphasising, since it provides an essential element of the
picture. The constitution had become democratic, but without
fracturing the central authority historically possessed by the
Crown. A transfer had taken place, from Crown to Parliament
(and thereby to people), but 'this curious process, by which the
personal authority of the King has been turned into the sovereignty of the King in Parliament, has had two effects: it has put
an end to the arbitrary powers of the monarch; and it has preserved intact and undiminished the supreme authority of the
State.'[10] In other words, democracy had not pluralized or diffused
power, merely shifted its location and legitimacy. State power
had not been compromised, but rather had found a new basis in
modern conditions. This 'curious' fact was a further ingredient of
British distinctiveness; and a further cause for satisfaction.

It is right to take Dicey seriously – and not just because of the profound influence of his account in shaping a twentieth-century doctrine of the constitution. He provides an indispensable reference point for subsequent discussion. The easy symmetry of his account was itself an example of a political tradition which refused to take democracy too seriously, for he was able to demonstrate that it had been effortlessly absorbed by a constitution which had not been fundamentally altered in the process. It was, in practical terms, a people's constitution, even if formal doctrines and institutions suggested otherwise, and despite the fact that the people (and their rights) enjoyed no formal place in the constitutional sun. In fact, of course, Dicey's account was too easy and, as it turned out, dangerously misleading as a description of the requirements of democratic politics. Indeed, if we turn from Dicey the academic lawyer of the constitution to Dicey the Liberal Unionist activist, it is striking to observe the political and constitutional contrast. The former had provided compelling grounds for believing that a sovereign Parliament would always bow to the wishes of a sovereign people; the latter argued that it did nothing of the kind. For it was Dicey who denounced the way in which a small and temporary Commons majority could 'arrogate to itself that legislative omnipotence which of right belongs to the nation' and insisted (in the context of the 1911 Parliament Act) that 'no country, except England, now dreams of placing itself under the rule of a single elected House'.[11] He had earlier warned that 'against this abuse of temporary power democrats must always be on their guard' and advocated the referendum as a device of conservative democracy to check the power of the Commons ('a democratic check on democratic evils').[12]

It is not necessary to agree with Dicey's politics, or with his favoured remedy, to think that these anxieties take us closer to some of the democratic dilemmas of the constitution than his more celebrated analysis. Others had anxieties too, of course (as with Ostrogorski's account of the development of the organized party system),[13] but it was the celebratory analysis which became the twentieth century norm. This suggested that the British constitution had made a successful democratic adaptation and that it was rooted in a series of 'understandings' which reflected and secured its democratic character. The balance of the constitution had shifted decisively towards the Commons, on which the executive was dependent, and the Commons was itself the effective creature of the electorate (though mediated by an established understanding about the proper nature of representation). The legal sovereignty of Parliament really meant the political sovereignty of the electorate, and democracy was thereby secured. This had been accomplished without, and did not require, any new constitutional settlement. Indeed, the traditional authority of the state had not been eroded, merely its basis altered.

Here was a model of the constitution that could easily be adapted and adopted in the world of organized party competition and mass electorate which developed after the First World War and continued thereafter. It was not designed for such a world, but came to fit it admirably. In particular, it could be converted into a party model, whereby political parties representing sections of the electorate acquired mandates to rule through electoral competition on the basis of manifestos and programmes. The democratic sovereignty of the electorate was expressed as the ability of a majority party to secure control of a sovereign Parliament and to rule without let or hindrance (though with proper regard to the constitutional conventions). It is not surprising that the parties found this view of the constitution – and of democracy – congenial, especially as it was buttressed (in the case of the two parties that mattered) by their own ideological dispositions. Nor is it surprising that little more was heard, at least not for a very long time, of those early century notes of doubt and dissent. The model of disciplined parties using the opportunities afforded by a 'flexible' constitution to press their ideological purposes on the basis of transient electoral victories was a million miles away from Dicey's description of a constitution made democratic by a particular relationship between Commons and people. Yet Dicey's account of the constitution had opened a door through which others could eagerly and effortlessly pass.

Perhaps Tocqueville knew better after all. Perhaps it did make more sense to regard a constitution that could be altered at will by a sovereign Parliament as no constitution at all. It was a constitution without either a defined relationship between the organs of state and their powers or a definition of the rights of citizenship, the twin components of constitutionalism. No distinction was made, and no special procedures were involved, to separate constitutional laws from ordinary legislation. The emphasis on custom and convention was another way of saying that the constitution was made up as it went along. Moreover, it was made up within a governing tradition which had retained the prerogatives and powers of the Crown and had passed these less to Commons and people (as Dicey suggested) and more, in a modern context, to party governments and executives.

The effect was to produce a particular kind of political system and a particular kind of politics. Its distinctiveness was proudly proclaimed and robustly celebrated by most of its participants (and observers at home and abroad) for much of this century. It seemed to work; it combined political stability with democratic party competition, and its understandings were widely understood. There is an interesting passage in Herbert Morrison's congratulatory account of the British political system (based upon his experience as a leading figure in the 1945–51 Labour Government) in which he explains why governments should avoid highly controversial legislation and 'play the game' required by parliamentary democracy if representative government was not to be endangered.[14] The notion of 'playing the game' as the basis of the political system is very significant, making it a matter of internal norms and élite political culture. The question is whether this is an adequate basis for a modern system of democratic government. Indeed, doubts have arisen whether the game is still being played, at least by gentlemen, or even whether anyone can remember the rules any more.

Dicey had made democracy too easy, and too simple. Without knowing it, or liking it, he had provided a view of the constitution which enabled democracy to become a matter of political parties claiming mandates to rule on the basis of electoral (or, more precisely, parliamentary) majorities, in a context where the restraints on ruling were meagre and informal. The point is not that political parties, even organised and disciplined ones, should not seek to advance their ideological objectives through the electoral and governing process. It is essential to democratic politics that they should. The point is that this is not an adequate account of the requirements of democratic governance, yet the British constitutional tradition has too easily allowed it to seem so.

Here, too, Tocqueville had a larger sense of what was properly involved, certainly if democracy was not to be merely majoritarianism, which is why he paid attention to the ways in which power could be pluralized and democratic liberty defended. Democracy is a claim to power, based upon equal political (and, for some, social) rights; and it is also a claim about the way in which such power should be exercised. Hence, on one side, it is about issues of participation and representation; and, on the other side, about such matters as accountability and openness. In Britain, though, it was much more a matter of a political fix, an adjustment to a governing tradition with an established constitutional pedigree. Thus Dicey was able to explain that, curiously, democracy had changed everything, yet everything remained the same. If, at the end of the twentieth century, observers of the British constitution draw attention to its 'grotesque imbalance'[15] against democracy, that imbalance is an authentic expression of a much longer history of constitutional thought and practice.

4

Dominocracy

Did anyone . . . envisage when this government was elected what staggering accumulations of power would be assembled at the centre?

Hugo Young *Guardian* (3 July 1990)

The time has come to introduce Professor Dicey to Mr Guy. Professor Dicey, as we have seen, had no difficulty in explaining that the potential for tyranny implied by the legal sovereignty of Parliament was nullified by the political sovereignty of the electorate, buttressed by a political culture in which everybody played by the rules. It has been well said that 'at the heart of Dicey's faith in parliamentary sovereignty was his belief that English gentlemen would only pass morally acceptable laws'.[1] Or behave, at least politically, in morally acceptable ways.

Now consider the case of John Guy, consultant orthopaedic surgeon at Worcester Royal Infirmary, who wrote to the patients on his waiting list to tell them that they could not have their hip operations because of the financial cuts in the health district, going on to suggest that they take the matter up with their Members of Parliament. One woman duly wrote to Nicholas Ridley, then Secretary of State for the Environment, who responded by despatching a sharp note to Health Minister, Tony Newton:

She encloses a letter from the consultant in Worcester, which is a circular urging all such patients to complain about what he describes as the deplorable situation. It seems to me intolerable that employees of the Health Service should openly criticise their health authorities and the Government in this sort of way. I would be glad if you could investigate this and see that the necessary action is taken to silence Mr Guy.[2]

It will be recalled that the same Mr (later, Lord) Ridley who wanted to 'silence Mr Guy' was also one of the most robust defenders of the sovereignty of Parliament as the hallmark of British democracy.

The point is not *ad hominem*; the example not singular. What matters is the tone, for this captures the inherent authoritarianism of a system and style of government which is remarkably free of effective checks and balances, and where a democratic legitimacy has been acquired by a traditional executive power. Of course, all states are inherently authoritarian – that is what the monopoly of force claimed by states is all about – and many states are visibly and brutally authoritarian. The British case is of a different order, so secure in its historic possession of the appertunances of democratic liberty that a low-grade process of erosion can take place without ever reaching a critical moment and avoiding any engagement with fundamentals. In a similar way, it may be said, the Thatcher years were a special case, ideologically driven, repudiating consensus-building and an old politics of understandings, and acquiring the inevitable ruling arrogance that accompanies repeated electoral victories and a prolonged period of office.

There is much truth in this. The mistake, though, would be to identify the special character of the Thatcher period, but to miss the general character of the political system which provided its essential setting. It is simply not possible to understand Thatcherism without also understanding that it was in Britain, uniquely among the Western democracies, that it could both take the form it did and be sustained for so long. There was no electoral system to prevent a party with only a minority of support sweeping the board; no effective second chamber to curb the excesses of a Commons majority; no written constitution to set the parameters of legitimate action; no constitutionally secure system of subnational government to prevent the centre riding roughshod over local and regional power; no charter of the basic rights of citizenship against which legislation had to be measured; no constitutional court to which appeal could be made on matters of constitutional propriety or the infringements of citizenship; no laws to open up public access to official information. This catalogue of negatives can be restated as a formidable positive: a system of government which is democratically distinctive in its concentration, centralization and secrecy. Its presiding spirit is not that of *demos* but of *dominus*. It may properly be called a dominocracy.

It is a top-down, executive-dominated way of governing. This has often been recognized, though traditionally held to be both benign and beneficial. Benign because the system was in the hands of gentlemen; beneficial because it enabled governments to govern. Sometimes its essence was distilled wrongly, even by those who aspired to emulate it, classically so by those eighteenth-century observers like Montesquieu who thought its guarantee of liberty was to be found in a separation of power and missed its actual fusion. More accurately, they identified an actual separation of power, but confused this political fact with a constitutional system of checks and balances. When Blackstone proclaimed as 'the true excellence of the English constitution, that all the parts of it form a mutual check upon each other',[3] this was a plausible characterization of the balance of power between the Crown and two Houses of Parliament bequeathed by the settlement of 1689. But this was a fact of politics and history, not a constitutional fundamental. Indeed, he warned of the potential for tyranny if one element came to dominate. Yet the checks and balances have now largely disappeared, leaving single-chamber government controlled by ministers wielding both executive and legislative power. In Lord Scarman's words, 'we have achieved that total union of executive and legislative power which Blackstone foresaw would be productive of tyranny.'[4]

It is true, of course, that this development is a consequence of democracy; but it is also a problem for democracy. This is especially so in a country where democracy has meant little more than the graft of an extended franchise and elective politics onto the structure of an existing constitution. It has been the means whereby a traditional and pre-democratic set of checks and balances has been eroded, but it has not, yet, been the means whereby a new set has come to be established. It is not a matter of restoring the old ones, nor a question of calling in the constitution to provide protection against democratic majorities. It is, rather, a matter of thinking through the kind of democracy appropriate to the government of a complex modern state. Of course this is not easy or straightforward. It is just that in Britain it is harder than it need be. It has been made harder still, and more urgent, by a recently prevailing ideology which is not merely dismissive of such concerns, but manages to dissolve them. When, in 1988, a debate was initiated in the House of Lords on the concentration and centralization of power, the revealing response from the government (in the shape of the Lord Advocate of Scotland, Lord Cameron of Lochbroom) was to point to the diffusion of power through the 'democratic institutions of the market place and the price mechanism'.[5] We shall have to return to this contemporary privatization of politics.

The constitution is unbalanced, and what remains of a play-the-game political culture can no longer disguise the fact. There is a British tradition of invoking the informal polity as a substitute for the structural idiosyncracies of the formal polity. Because there was a custom-and-practice constitution there was no need to write it down. Because governments toed the line there was no necessity to build walls along it. Because power was diffused in practice there was no advantage in having formal safeguards against centralization. This mode of argument has sustained a dangerously misleading self-image. For example, it has been possible to believe that the British polity was distinguished by a high degree of institutional pluralism, whereas it is actually distinguished by a marked absence of a plurality of centres of power and an extraordinary degree of concentration.

There is a further twist to this story. In the case of the institutions of local democracy, as Miller has put it, it has been a matter of 'expecting local government to substitute for the *lack of a constitution* and for the *lack of an institutional system of checks and balances*'.[6] The informal constitution was invoked as a surrogate for a formal constitution. Local government, in particular, was therefore presented as having a larger constitutional significance beyond its role in providing local services. At least, it was so presented until a government thought otherwise and used its actual powers to kick away this central support of the British informal constitution. Whatever else this did, it provided a cold douche of political reality to those still basking in the reflective glow of old stories told by the fire in the constitutional longroom.

More generally, recent British politics have removed any lingering excuse for not grasping the character of a dominocracy. This is where rulers are too powerful; where there are inadequate means of challenge, scrutiny and accountability; and political life itself, as well as the quality of citizenship, is eroded and devalued. It is not necessary to give a chronicle of the events of recent years or a roll call of the *causes célèbres* to see what is involved. Public lawyers have amply documented 'the extent to which core political freedoms have been compromised'[7] by the recent actions of government on a range of fronts. A special edition of the authoritative *Index on Censorship*, the first edition ever devoted to a Western democracy, has charted the wave of assaults on 'the state of freedom' in Britain during the 1980s.[8] A leading judge (Mr Justice Scott, in the context of injunctions against newspapers in the *Spycatcher* case) has spoken in court of the government of the day advancing a position which he had not expected to see 'this side of the Iron Curtain'.[9] Britain has an unenviable record as the best customer at the European Court of Human Rights.

The point, at least for present purposes, is not whether the particular actions of government are wise or wicked. There may be a case for seeking, in certain circumstances, to prosecute journalists or civil servants, for wanting publications suppressed or films not shown. There will be legitimate argument about how security services should be controlled, terrorism dealt with, the police organized, public order maintained, official secrets kept, telephones tapped. Widening the field, there may be good reasons for wanting to nationalize education, turn health into a market, or introduce a poll tax. What is wrong is a system of government in which such things may be done simply because the government wants to do them, and where, having jumped the single obstacle of election, the way is largely clear of either obstacle or argument. The parliamentary troops are whipped into duty to perform their legitimating routine. A winner-takes-all electoral system goes hand in hand with a winner-takes-all system of government. Parliamentary sovereignty is another way of saying that governments, a few hiccups apart, get what they want. Little wonder, then, that governments display such ardour in defending it against those, whether at home or abroad, who would tamper with it.

Yet governing is too important to be left to governments; and politics too important to be left to politicians. The alternative is a corruption of public life of the kind that Britain began to experience during the Thatcher years. Not merely bad laws (of which the poll tax will long stand as the outstanding example), bad because uninformed by evidence and untested by scrutiny,[10] but a kind of politics in which any distinction between a public interest and the interests of those in power is increasingly obscured and denied. This, it will be recalled, was precisely the line of reasoning deployed by the Thatcher government in its approach to security issues, both in the courts and in legislation, and it was a line of constitutional argument which an executive-minded judiciary (as in Mr Justice McCowan's celebrated identification of the public interest with the government's interest) has shown itself more than ready to endorse. It is also a kind of politics in which ministers feel no need to consult a wider constituency of interests, or establish independent channels of inquiry and advice, in framing legislation. These, too, were traditionally cited as one of the informal pillars of the constitution; but they also found themselves swept aside as the accretions of a 'corporatism' which dared to suggest that governing was a complex and negotiated process in which there were many legitimate interests.

Thus ministers decide. They may decide, as they did in a single week, to impose a broadcasting ban and end the right to silence in criminal cases. They may decide to abolish a level of local government, abolish the government of London, and take sweeping powers to curb and control the rest of the local government system. They may decide to kick out those members of health authorities not palatable to their political taste and replace them from the centre with their own appointees. They may decide that trade unionists who want to strike must hold a ballot, but that trusts who want to opt out of the local health service should not. They may decide to strip local education authorities of their powers, and they may decide what kind of history should be taught in schools. They may decide that businessmen should run the universities and the schools and the health services. They may decide to change the way in which official statistics are collected and presented, and to control the way in which research for government departments is reported. They may decide to create ever larger spaces in parliamentary bills to be filled by their discretionary powers. They may lubricate the whole system with a generosity of patronage unequalled, in the case of the Thatcher government, since Lloyd George's sale of the century.

They may, and they have. The contingencies of a period (a dominant prime minister, an enfeebled opposition, a rampant ideology) should not obscure the characteristics of a system. It brings with it its own style of politics. It is a style in which persuasion and argument count for little, a politics of watching and consuming rather than engaging and sharing, a politics for subjects rather than for citizens. If it produces a weary and cynical disengagement on the part of the electorate – what was described in the mid-1980s as 'a poverty of expectation on the part of the entire British electorate'[11] – it produces an equally weary and cynical arrogance on the part of governments. The recent period is the more revealing precisely because it was heralded as the period when the deplorable 'growth in government over the last quarter of a century' (in the words of the 1979 Conservative manifesto) would be hauled in and disciplined.

Instead, it has served to throw the essential character of a system into sharp relief, which no subsequent softening should be allowed to obscure. It finds its real expression and epitaph in that ministerial directive to 'silence Mr Guy'.

5

Doubts and discontents

Democracy has itself by the tail and is eating itself up fast.

Peter Jay *Englanditis* (1977)

When, in 1989, Lady Ewart-Biggs wrote to Margaret Thatcher on behalf of Charter 88, the campaign for constitutional reform, soliciting support for measures designed to strengthen the citizen against the state, the response from the then Prime Minister was as predictable as it was untroubled. 'The government consider', she wrote, 'that our present constitutional arrangements continue to serve us well.' The identity of 'us' remained elusive. Certainly it continued to serve governments and ministers well, investing them with a massive concentration of power and protecting them from effective discipline in their use of it. It was not so clear, except to those like Mrs Thatcher, that this kind of system continued to serve the rest of us very well.

So there is an issue. But we need to take a few paces backwards before trying to edge even half a step forward in thinking about it. It is necessary, in other words, to say something about the origins of present discontents. These may be dated, at least in their modern form, from the 1970s, when a comfortable complacency about the British way of governing suddenly found itself replaced by a profound anxiety. Those who had earlier wanted to celebrate the British system as the paradigm of good government now joined the queue of those who wanted – with varying degrees of emphasis – to pronounce that something was wrong, even that what was wrong represented the contemporary paradigm of wrongness in the matter of government.[1] This was a remarkable change. From a situation where the description was of a model of stable, two-party politics delivering what people wanted, requiring only the occasional modernizing jerk (a select committee system here, a bit of local government or civil service reform there), there had developed a wide-ranging critique of the infirmities and disabilities of the British political system and its ideological underpinnings.

It was a system where the participants had hitherto averted any engagement with fundamentals, taking great care to ensure that the need to negotiate particular problems did not provoke any larger constitutional inquiry. Issues were diligently ring-fenced. Thus the grandly named Royal Commission on the Constitution (which reported in 1973) was really a misnomer, confining its attention strictly to the Celtic matter in hand. The Fulton Committee on the Civil Service (reporting in 1968) was likewise constrained by narrow terms of reference from trespassing into such serious constitutional territory as ministerial responsibility, just as the Redcliffe-Maud Commission on Local Government (reporting in 1969) was confined to an examination of existing structures and functions. What was intended was a series of separate modernizing initiatives, not a systematic and principled process of institutional modernization. It has similarly been observed that the story of the development of public law and administrative justice in Britain has involved a resolute refusal to take stock of the nature of government as a whole. Rather, it has been a matter of systematic ad-hocery, the piecemeal inquiry and the 'quick political response', the result of which is 'an unco-ordinated hotchpotch'.[2]

This is what it means not to take the modern state, or democracy, seriously. Much better to settle for good old British muddling through and to practice a politics of containment in relation to potentially unsettling issues. During the 1970s, though, there was demonstrably more muddle than through, as industrial politics threatened to shipwreck an ailing economy and take the polity down with it. The ills of the economy were routine fare for analysis; what was new was the attention now given to the political system. Indeed, more even than this, there was the attempt from a number of directions to make the polity the cause rather than the consequence of social and economic ills.[3] For some this meant an identification of a British system of 'adversary politics' as the villain of the piece, the damaging source of policy reversals and the failure to construct durable institutions. Gone was the celebration of the British model of alternating two-party government. For others the problem was one of governmental 'overload', where government was swamped and overwhelmed by the pressure of demands, interests and expectations on it and lacked the capacity to deliver. In part, this kind of analysis – which rapidly became a new orthodoxy – was intended as a general account of the difficulties of Western governments as a whole; but it was in relation to Britain that the analysis, with its febrile anticipation of systemic breakdown, was intended to have its most compelling application. It was not always made clear why this should be so, except for the fact that contemporary events seemed to provide evidence enough that governing Britain had become a peculiarly difficult enterprise.

What is of particular interest, though, is the way in which this line of argument (again with Britain as the exemplary case) was theorized as a general problem of democracy. More precisely, democracy *was* the problem. It generated excessive and inconsistent expectations, stoked the fires of inflation, produced a battery of interest group pressures, induced politicians to do what was politically expedient rather than economically desirable, and extended the improper hand of government into areas where it should not decently reach. What looked like the British economic problem was really the British political problem. As Samuel Brittan explained:

> To escape our predicament, we need not another revolution in economic theory, but a revolution in constitutional and political ideas which will save us from the snare of unlimited democracy, before we find ourselves with no democracy – and very little freedom – left.[4]

What made Britain distinctive was an egalitarian, social democratic ideology – reflected in 'its obsession with interpersonal and intergroup comparisons'[5] – which made both economic and political problems much worse than they need be.

It should be noticed that this kind of argument was firmly located in that much longer tradition of anti-democratic thought identified earlier. This was the 1970s; but it had also been heard in the 1870s. At best, on this view, democracy was a problem requiring proper political management. It should also be noticed, though, that proponents of this view affirmed what was often denied, namely that democracy was not simply a matter of certain political arrangements, but was inextricably connected with larger ideological issues. Indeed, it was precisely because it was so contaminated with ideas about equality, fairness and social justice that democracy was said to pose such difficulties. Thus radicals of both right and left were in agreement on this, with only liberals in the middle believing the word to mean something else.

Nor were these merely academic arguments. They were an essential ingredient of the climate of ideas within which the Thatcher Government came to power in 1979 and an active constituent of the new right ideology which drove Thatcherism. The task that had been identified was a reduction both in the pressure of interests on government and in popular expectations of government, accompanied by a restriction and withdrawal of government from areas where it had no business. This was in every sense an ideological project, not merely an assault on a contemporary definition of the role of government, but an assault on the ideological underpinnings of that definition. Some thought that this project would require, and be the harbinger of, a new constitutional settlement; an ideological resolution in favour of the market accompanied by a new constitution to discipline government and restrict it to its proper business.[6] That this did not happen is another important part of the story.

What did happen, of course, was a resolute deployment of the formidable resources available to a British government to advance its ideological mission, even if this was still described in terms of the language of a rolled-back state. As one of Mrs Thatcher's intellectual allies put it: 'It is not the least of the paradoxes of her period of rule that the project of diminishing government has often led to an actual increase in the range of government intervention.'[7] Others have wanted to describe this paradox more robustly, drawing upon it to construct a contemporary case for radical constitutional reform to hold governments in check. There is an interesting development here. An argument that British government is too weak, overwhelmed by interests and pressures and excessive expectations, has been replaced by an argument that British government is too strong, able to cut down interest groups and ignore public opinion. Both arguments, despite being diametrically opposite, have sustained programmes of radical institutional reform of a remarkably similar kind, though with equal lack of serious political endorsement.

They have also sustained a misleadingly false antithesis. Either you have the kind of corporatist bog which brought government to its knees in the 1970s or you have the kind of gung-ho, none-

of-this-consensus-nonsense government which was the hallmark
of the 1980s; there is nothing in between. The tragedy is that, in
Britain, there *has* been so little in between, beyond a game-playing
political culture. Thus the Thatcher Government found it relatively easy to cut a swathe through popular expectations[8] and
scythe down those intermediate institutions associated with a rival
network of interests. This was warmly applauded by those who
had urged just such a course as the way of saving democracy
from itself, and who could therefore scarcely complain about a
system of government which made this task easier than it should
have been in the light of their own earlier analysis, or which
accumulated many new powers for itself along the way. They
might acknowledge a certain 'paradox' in what had happened, but
not the means whereby it had happened. Their greater difficulty
came in explaining why their recommended mode of government
had not produced either the cultural revolution or the economic
transformation which had also been an essential part of the prospectus.

Another paradox, or rather two, involved those other people
who had concluded from this same period and process that British
governments had too much unaccountable power at their disposal
and needed reining in. New recruits to this view (notably Charter
88, with its demands for a new constitutional settlement involving
a written constitution, bill of rights and a reformed electoral
system) were precisely the people who were traditionally well
disposed towards big government and wanted to extend its range
of activities in pursuance of desirable social and economic objectives. Thus the new disposition of forces found the ideological
opponents of government interference embracing the virtues of a
system that enabled robust governments to interfere all over the
place, while the ideological exponents of interfering government
assembled behind a set of demands designed to inhibit the scope
for such interference.

If not quite a paradox, there was certainly a further tension in
this latter position. It was not clear whether what was being
proposed was a change in the political environment within which
British government operated (though probably needing a more
proportional electoral system to secure this) or a more fundamental alteration in the constitutional basis of government in Britain.
Not only were these different, but they might well be seen as
alternatives. If the problem was that British governments were too

powerful because the political restraints (party balance, electoral competition, political culture) had become weaker, then the remedies were of a similarly political kind (a more effective opposition, closer run elections, a more consensual political culture). However, if the problem was identified as more systemic and fundamental, then an equally radical and far-reaching response would be required, one which went beyond any adjustment to the prevailing political environment.

For most people, of course, there was no problem of any kind (beyond the need, in politicians' terms, to win the next election). Those who regarded democracy as a 'snare' liked that version of it which could so easily break free from popular pressures. Those who regarded it as the majoritarian mobilization of such pressures likewise looked with favour on a system which placed remarkably few formal obstacles in the way of majority rule. The fact that there could be such congruence between contrasting ideological positions suggests the need to think about democracy rather differently, as a way of keeping an effective check on what Hirst calls 'continuously functioning big government'.[9] The size and scope of modern government, irrespective of ideological self-descriptions (thus the size of government, measured in terms of public spending, rose not fell during the Thatcher years), requires a democratic response as diverse and extensive as government itself, going wider and deeper than the mechanisms and categories devised in relation to the very different nature of government in the nineteenth century. Government has marched on; democracy, broadly speaking, has not kept in step.

It is right that government has marched on. We need it to do great things and slay great giants on our behalf, to enable us to do collectively what we cannot do individually, to realise shared purposes and values. Those who want to roll back the state are usually not only partial in the bits they want to roll back, but frequently attack the agent to conceal the object. What is, and should be, an argument about ends is dressed up as an argument about means. But the means do matter; and should matter most to those who most want the ends. Big government needs to be effective, and it needs to be democratic.[10] If we do want it to slay giants for us, we had better make sure both that it slays them effectively and that it remains under the firm control of the master on whose behalf it is supposed to be doing the slaying.

This, it is suggested, is what the current arguments ought to be about (and, in part at least, are); and especially so in Britain. This, too, is why there is a false antithesis between the corporatist tinkering of the 1970s and the smack of firm government of the 1980s, for the lack of democratic institution-building is the missing part of the story. If there seemed to be a problem of legitimacy in both those periods, it was because there was precisely such a problem, and little thought was given to the means whereby legitimacy might be acquired for government and its activities on a continuing basis. The recent demand to constitutionalize British government is an oddly old-fashioned demand, explicable in terms of an odd constitutional and political history but, at best, necessary rather than sufficient as an account of a contemporary project of democratization in relation to the 'extended political system'[11] with which we are faced. It is at least a nice irony, though, that one of the unanticipated consequences of Thatcherism has been a renewed and radical attention to the political system which made it possible.

6

Representative government revisited

It is not because a part of the government is elective, that makes it less a despotism, if the persons so elected possess afterwards, as a parliament, unlimited powers. Election, in this case, becomes separated from representation, and the candidates are candidates for despotism.

Tom Paine *The Rights of Man* (1791)

We ought, then, to be developing democracy in relation to modern extended government. Instead, we inhabit a political tradition which makes this an exceptionally difficult enterprise. A range of venerable doctrines are marshalled to explain why matters are organized as they are, undeterred by the ever more yawning gap between what the doctrines proclaim and what the contemporary practices demonstrate. Nowhere is this more evident than with the doctrine of representation.

It is a doctrine that should have been extended and enriched in line with extended government and the needs of a complex democracy. Not only did this not happen, but even tentative and informal steps in this direction have been brushed away and a traditional doctrine reasserted with the vigour needed to conceal its ossification. The stark truth is that British government lacks a convincing theory of representation, convincing in the sense that it corresponds to what actually happens. The lack of such a theory is not new, nor the identification of a mismatch between a nineteenth century doctrine of representation and its twentieth century reality. However, a generation ago the lack of a justificatory theory could both be noted and dismissed as yet another example of that typically British ability to muddle through: 'The system works, and those who understand it are mostly content to accept it.'¹ What is new is that it does not work, at least in the terms once claimed for it; and its ability to win acceptance – even among 'those who understand it' – has markedly diminished.

Let us get our bearings. Representation was 'the grand discovery of modern times'², upon which a modern theory of the constitution could be constructed. It was not a democratic discovery, as an earlier doctrine of 'virtual' representation testified, but it was the great modern bridge to democracy. It explained how the people could rule without actually ruling and how governments could be made to serve a general interest rather than their own particular interest. There was room for argument about the organization of a system of representative government (as with John Stuart Mill)³ but not about its essential rightness or desirability. The progressive enlargement of the franchise could be seen as a process of squaring the democratic circle in terms of representation. The people would rule through representatives freely chosen by means of elections in which all were entitled to participate.

So there emerged a modern theory of the constitution anchored in a doctrine of representation. It was democratic, in the sense that it was rooted in a process of election involving (eventually) the whole adult population. It was also liberal, in the sense both that it presented the business of representation in individualistic terms and emphasised the independence of the individual representative against the claims of mandating and delegation. It issued in the comfortable orthodoxy of parliamentary sovereignty, underpinned by representative democracy, as the self-declared foundation stone of the whole system. It was also quite misleading as a guide to what was actually happening, even at the beginning of this century when its truths were being confidently proclaimed. It became even more misleading as the century progressed, as the party system tightened its grip on the polity and enforced its own view of the nature of representation. Elections ceased to be about the selection of individual representatives exercising their judgements in a sovereign Parliament (as traditional doctrine asserted) and became a matter of parties organizing the electorate to produce disciplined majorities able to dominate Parliament in the service of governments.

The new practice borrowed what it needed from the old theory (not least the doctrine of parliamentary sovereignty) and appearances were kept up for as long as decently possible (thus it was only relatively recently – since the General Election of 1970 – that party affiliations were even identified on ballot papers), but this could not disguise what had happened. Indeed, it could quite properly be seen as a necessary development, a collectivist twist to an originally liberal view of representation in response to a new alignment of social forces and the new tasks of government. Equally properly, the new dispensation equipped itself with an appropriate ideology of electoral mandates and manifesto politics to underpin the view of representation implied in the model of organized party competition to form governments on a programmatic basis. Moreover, both the character of the electoral system and the nature of electoral behaviour could be seen (most visibly in the middle decades of the twentieth century) as perfectly congruent with this representative model. A two-party system seemed rooted in – and the expression of – a competitive struggle between parties representing class blocs which defined the entire electorate (for a quarter of a century after 1945 the combined Conservative and Labour vote scarcely dipped below 90 per cent) and an electoral system which translated this social and political bi-polarity into sharp alternatives, clear majorities and strong governments. An electoral system without the individualist distractions of rigid proportionality enabled a society to give effect to its essential character and to make its collective choices.

It is important to emphasise the sound historical credentials of this post-liberal, collectivist, twentieth-century view of representation precisely because it has now broken down. It no longer fits the facts, but nothing has yet taken its place. For a long time, and in some quarters, the main threat to it was seen to come from those who wanted to tamper with its remaining liberal ingredients by pressing a view of representation which sought to diminish the independence of elected representatives by increasing the power of the extra-parliamentary party. This was the standing charge against Labour made by the Conservatives and has been a recurrent motif in Labour's own history. It was natural that this should be so, since Labour carried from its trade union origins a delegate view of representation which had to find a mode of co-existence (formally enshrined in the Party's constitution) with its parliamentary version. The issue erupted again in the 1980s and nearly sank the Labour Party in the process (and might still yet, if trade union resistance thwarts democratic reform).

It is worth recalling this bloody period because of the light it throws on the matter of representation. In the name of democracy it was demanded that the parliamentary Labour Party should, through a variety of means, be made to follow more closely the wishes of the Party's rank-and-file. Presented as an extension of democracy, this was really its contraction. By making elected members more representative of party activists, the effect was to make them *less* representative of everybody else (including the Party's own wider membership).[4] One of the most revealing, and least edifying, aspects of this period was the way in which democratic tribunes of the left, such as Tony Benn, found ingenious reasons for opposing the wider enfranchisement of the Party's members.

The episode serves as a reminder of the perils of attempting to reconstruct a view of representation on shaky foundations. In particular, it highlights the error of seeking to elevate a party model of representation at precisely the moment when the basis for such a model is being eroded and in urgent need of reinforcement from other directions. Election studies reveal the diminished salience of party, both in terms of affiliation and its social supports, and the emergence of a more variegated pattern of political allegiance and behaviour.[5] The age of the mass party, the creature of the democratic franchise and of classical ideological politics, may anyway be drawing to a close. Parties are indispensable vehicles for the organization of political choice; but they do not exhaust the range of representative possibilities.

For these and other reasons, we now have a political system which is living off its capital. Whereas it was once possible to argue that the electoral system reflected the essential character of British politics, for the last two decades it would be more accurate to say that it is only the electoral system which has propped up British politics in its traditional form.[6] That may be thought to be good or bad, but what is not in doubt is the price in representational terms that has had to be paid for it (and in other terms too). British governments have claimed more and more on the basis of less and less. The Thatcher revolution of the 1980s was made on the back of huge parliamentary majorities corresponding to levels of electoral support which would have lost elections only a few decades earlier. Ever more people (not just those voting for the smaller parties) have been effectively disenfranchised as electoral geography reduces the number of marginal seats and increases the mountain of wasted votes. In ever more constituencies it is the candidate selection process (confined to the small flock of doubtfully representative party faithful) rather than the general election itself which constitutes the decisive election. Put all this together and it is not surprising that a rough calculation reveals that Britain is now bottom of the international league table in terms of representativeness of its governments.[7]

When the television cameras arrived, finally, in the House of Commons, the extent to which a further version of representation – that version which looks for social similarities between representative and represented – was conspicuous by its absence was also starkly illuminated. Starkest of all was the absence of women (even more so those with families) among all those pink-cheeked merchant bankers and freshly filofaxed trade union officials; an absence on a scale really requiring a modern version of the doctrine of virtual representation to do it full justice. The parties have responded to their embarrassment on this matter by trying to fix the party system a little (hence the brouhaha of the black candidate parachuted into Cheltenham by the Conservative Party), lest anyone should think that there is something more fundamentally amiss with a representative system that produces such consistently unrepresentative consequences. In case there is doubt whether this version of representation matters, it is only necessary to recall Aristotle's remarks on those who best know where the shoe pinches.

In general terms, the kind of story that could be told in explanation and support of the British representative system during the period between 1945 and 1974 no longer carries conviction. It was then plausible to argue (notwithstanding a lack of precise mathematical fairness) that there was a broad 'fit' between a majoritarian and adversarial two-party political system and the disposition of issues, ideologies and classes. There is no longer such a fit, just as there is no regularly swinging pendulum to provide the alternating governments and oppositional politics which were traditionally advanced as the surrogates for more formal and institutionalized restraints on governments and more concertational ways of governing. Despite this lack of fit, the system is kept in business by an electoral system of ever increasing disproportionality and by the attachment to it of politicians who are its existing or putative beneficiaries. They may still claim to have mandates (never a convincing claim in policy terms anyway), but what they really have are just election victories. The fact of election, there-

fore, becomes the single hinge upon which the larger representative claims increasingly turn, so that the task becomes that of
adroit and 'professional' election management (aided in the case
of the governing party by its ability to choose the date). In this
way, representation ceases to be a continuous process, linking
governors and governed, and becomes the matter of a single
managed moment. As Paine put it, election becomes separated
from representation and the right to select representatives becomes
separated from the ability to control them.[8]

Instead of being extended in response to the character of big
government and a complex society, representation is thereby
narrowed to a primary identification with electoral politics (of an
unreconstructed kind) and the historical fact of universal suffrage.
It may be objected that this fails to take account of that whole
informal network of policy communities and interest structures
through which government actually operates[9], and which has traditionally been cited as an auxiliary and legitimate system of
representation (and even of incorporation). Yet this has enjoyed
no secure status and, in constitutional terms, has never come in
from the cold. Recent history amply demonstrates that what has
never been formally given can easily be taken away. Thus Keith
Ewing remarks on how, in the 1980s, the trade unions 'fell victim
to the flexible and open-ended nature of the constitution. Just as
their influence grew without any formal change to the structure
of the Westminster system, so they could be excluded in much
the same way.'[10] Indeed, what is significant is that the twentieth-
century growth in networks and structures connecting governments and interests was not accompanied by any sustained attempt
to translate this into a revised theory and practice of representation.

Instead there was a resolute defence of a traditional constitutional orthodoxy against those who sought to combine functional and territorial representation in new ways (as with the
proposal for an industrial parliament which made an intermittent
appearance). In the same way, proposals designed to supplement
broad electoral choice with specific policy choice, as with refer-
endums, have been consistently ruled out of court in constitutional
terms (except, of course, when they have proved useful in digging
parties out of a hole). The result is that we are left with an
increasingly threadbare doctrine of representation that, as J. A.
Hobson once remarked, merely involves the electorate in 'plung-

ing into a sensational sporting contest once in six years and registering a single vote upon a medley of personalities and party cries.'[11]

This may serve to legitimate what governments do (though less and less effectively) but it does not do much to represent people in their relations with power and the powerful. It reduces to a single choice, under arbitrary rules, what should be a continuous process. It compresses into a single channel what should be a differentiated activity. It enables some interests to be represented while others are excluded. What it does not do, as Dicey claimed, is to provide the means whereby an exceptionally powerful executive is translated, without the need for further devices, into a system of popular government. Nor does it address the question of the kind of representative structure appropriate to the government of late twentieth-century society if democracy is taken seriously. There is no straightforward answer; but that is no reason to go on pretending that there is no question either.

7

Responsible government revisited

It is slightly curious that 'responsibility' which originally stood for the amenability of the Crown and its servants to legislative control should have come to stand . . . for an assertion of the executive's independence of parliamentary control.

> G. Marshall and G. Moodie *Some Problems of the Constitution* (1959)

The line of constitutional argument, and orthodoxy, runs directly from representation to responsibility. The claim that British governments are anchored in a securely democratic basis of representation is conjoined with the claim that governments are continuously accountable, answerable, responsible (pick your word) to the elected representatives of the people for all their actions and inactions. If there is good reason to dispute the former claim, there is equal reason to take issue with the latter.

Yet the claim would seem to be rooted both in good constitutional theory and daily political practice. On one side, the doctrine of ministerial responsibility is there to be wheeled out as required to explain the proper nature of constitutional relationships. On another side, the quotidian round of parliamentary questions, legislative debates, division bells, committee deliberations and ministerial interrogations is there to provide the doctrine with its practical testimony. History may be summoned up, too, to remind us of the process whereby Parliament wrested power from the Crown, not least the 'power of the purse', and thereby decisively shifted the balance of the constitution by making the Crown's ministers responsible to the people's representatives. This process, so the story goes, eventually issued in the modern doctrines of responsibility, of ministers collectively responsible for what governments say and do (memorably summarized by Lord Melbourne as 'we must all tell the same story') and of ministers individually responsible to Parliament for the actions of their departments. These twin pillars of the doctrine confirmed the status of a sovereign Parliament. If ministries lost the confidence of Parliament they had to fall; if ministers lost the confidence of Parliament they had to go.

It is clear at once that we have entered the land of myth. A mid-nineteenth-century interlude was used to misunderstand the character of twentieth-century government. Constitutional doctrines were proclaimed which bore ever less relationship to developing political practices. Appearances were kept up, but the reality gap steadily widened (requiring the doctrines to work overtime). This explains the peculiar unreality of so much of what Parliament does. The speeches addressed to the empty green benches, the persuasive in pursuit of the unpersuadable, the permanent election campaign disguised as something else, the late-night lobby trooping in votes where the result is already known; all this perfectly explicable to the participants in terms of the real constitution, but wholly inexplicable to observers in terms of the formal one. The evident gap between what Parliament actually does (and how it does it) and what it might reasonably be expected to do no doubt accounts for the low popular esteem in which it is held.[1] What are usually described as the 'great parliamentary occasions' are clearly seen as poor compensation for routine supineness in the face of modern executives and party whips.

Form conflicts with substance. Procedurally, notwithstanding government control of its business, Parliament goes through the motions of doing one kind of job when it is really doing something quite different. It is a legislature which plainly does not legislate. Its control and scrutiny of government clearly does not add up to responsibility. Governments have to manage Parliament and Parliament bestows legitimacy on what governments do (notice how ministers frequently talk of 'Parliament' having approved measures, especially unpopular ones), but these are the insights of political science not of received constitutional doctrine. The answer may simply be to revise the doctrine, as the obsolete relic of a faded liberal era, in line with the 'what actually happens' constitution. Such revision emphasises the growth of party government and presents Parliament as the grand arena where the party battle is enacted and the decisive political choices are illuminated. On this view, British politics is a matter of government and opposition and this is what Parliament should reflect, without distractions or diversions.

This view has the merit of realism. It cuts through much antique constitutional waffle and gets to the heart of the matter. It raises proper doubts about whether it is even useful to speak of 'Parliament' in a collective sense at all. Enoch Powell has put this well:

> The House is not just a corporation and simply to talk about the House vis-à-vis the Government is a totally inadequate description. The House comprises parties and, for most of the purposes of the House, its partisan character overrides its corporate character.[2]

There speaks, significantly, one of the 'great parliamentarians' of modern times who, also significantly, in unholy alliance with that other great parliamentarian, Michael Foot, mounted the resistance campaign against those putative parliamentary reformers who wanted to strengthen Parliament's corporate capacity to hold governments to account. Great parliamentarians of left and right thus united to prevent any muddying of the partisan battlefield. Responsibility was a matter of governments governing and oppositions opposing. It should not be diluted in an elusive and inevitably fruitless search for other modes of responsibility. There could not be, nor should there be, any hankering after a mythical golden age of parliamentary government.

But the myths continue to sustain the doctrines that purport to describe a reality with which they have ever less connection. A doctrine of collective ministerial responsibility purports to describe a politics in which governments have to win the continuing support of Parliament for their actions and face the standing threat of the loss of that support. The reality is of routine majorities and whipped battalions. The more a government is in difficulty the more its troops rally to the flag, or, sometimes, take oppositional matters into their own hands. Neither the poll tax nor Mrs Thatcher met their nemesis on the floor of the House of Commons. Conservative Euro-rebellion is, above all, an issue of internal party management. In the entire period of Conservative government from mid-1979 to the present (mid-1993) there have been precisely seven Government defeats on the floor of the Commons – on two of these occasions MPs combined to vote themselves increased allowances, and on the most recent occasion, in July 1993, the Government was able to reverse its defeat on the Social Chapter part of the Maastricht ratification process by converting it into a confidence motion and invoking the prerogative of dissolution. Likewise, a doctrine of individual ministerial responsibility purports to describe a politics in which ministers are personally accountable for the activities of their departments and pay the price of resignation if things go wrong. The doctrine both carries a fiction (that ministers are actually responsible for what civil servants do) and plainly conflicts with a political reality in which ministers do not pay the price for administrative and political error, but are politically protected both from making any such payment and from the likelihood of errors coming to light. Ministers may resign, but this will now have much to do with the political embarrassment of their continued presence (as with Mr Ridley's remarks about Germans and Mrs Currie's about eggs) and little or nothing to do with administrative failings.[3]

At no time was this clearer than in September 1992, when one minister (Heritage Minister, David Mellor) resigned in circumstances that had nothing to do with his ministerial responsibilities, as did the junior Northern Ireland minister, Michael Mates, in June 1993, while another minister (Chancellor Norman Lamont) failed to resign in circumstances that had everything to do with the ignominious collapse of policies for which he was responsible. Political embarrassment killed the former, but saved the latter. When he did eventually go, against his will and nearly a year later, it was also for reasons of general political liability.

Procedural rhetoric pays obeisance to doctrines which have become empty shells. The front benches make ritual appeals for support in divisions where the result is already known (and where what matters is not to listen to arguments but to record votes), as though the doctrine of collective responsibility of ministries to Parliament was still alive and well. Similarly, ritual demands for ministerial resignations are routinely made by ministers-in-waiting to ministers-in-office without any expectation on either side that anything but old motions are being gone through. The fact that a different version of responsibility is now operative, certainly in practice and sometimes in theory, does not prevent the older constitutional orthodoxies from being called in aid. The difficulty is that the current version of responsibility, with its emphasis on the disciplined organization of government and opposition, is not merely a departure from an earlier version, but its complete reversal.[4] In parliamentary terms, it is really a doctrine of irresponsibility.

This is why the subject of parliamentary reform is, like the weather, always with us, and why, also like the weather, nothing very much ever gets done about it. It has generally been a matter of pressing another definition of Parliament's role, involving an enhanced scrutiny of government, alongside the adversarial and party version of what responsible government entails. Even though reformers have generally been careful to present their proposals as consistent with the essential character of British government, rejecting any suggestion of an alternative approach,[5] this has not prevented these proposals from getting firmly stuck in the constitutional mud. This has to be the verdict on the select committees, long the spearhead of reformist zeal and, in their various incarnations, the decisive means whereby parliamentary ineffectiveness in face of the executive was to be addressed. The latest (post-1979) raft of select committees was prefaced by this familiar lament from the House of Commons Select Committee on Procedure:

> The balance of advantage between Parliament and Government in the day-to-day working of the Constitution is now weighted in favour of the Government to a degree which arouses widespread anxiety and is inimical to the proper working of our parliamentary democracy.[6]

Whatever else they may have done (and, in the phrase usually employed, they have much 'useful work' to their credit), the select committees have certainly not redressed the balance of the constitution.

Nor could they. Their environment is that of a dominant executive and a legislature disciplined by partisanship. The doctrine of ministerial responsibility sets the limit on any serious exploration of the policy options and makers within departments lest the bureaucratic and political fictions are breached. What the Defence Select Committee's celebrated investigation of the Westland affair revealed was not how effective this parliamentary instrument had now become, but how little could be glimpsed of the basis upon which policies were being made before the door was slammed shut again and business as normal resumed.[7] Similarly, when President of the Board of Trade, Michael Heseltine, told the Commons in his coal closure statement that 'nobody believes that a Select Committee is a substitute for Government' (25 March 1993), he was making it clear that a select committee report – in this case from the Trade and Industry Select Committee – should not be seen as interfering with the serious business of governing. This does not mean that the committees should just be dismissed as idle work for idle hands,[8] but it does mean that it is unrealistic to regard them as the substitute for more effective and extensive forms of responsibility.

Indeed, it is already the case that scrutiny is most effective where Parliament has equipped itself with the machinery appropriate to the task. It has long been recognized that the 'power of the purse' is something of a poor joke when set alongside the actual ability of Parliament to exercise financial accountability,[9] but it is also recognized that the ability of the Public Accounts Committee to scrutinize government departments, in a different league from other select committees, is rooted in the service provided to it by the National Audit Office of the Comptroller and Auditor-General (and the backing of the Treasury). The general lesson here is that if 'responsibility' is largely nullified in practice, whatever constitutional doctrine may say, by the partisan structure of the Commons, then rather than expect Parliament to undertake functions it is unlikely to be able to perform (certainly in its unreformed condition), it may be more sensible to look to Parliament to establish other methods and machinery whereby effective responsibility can be secured.

At present, we have a traditional doctrine of responsibility which has become a political fiction, and a more realistic doctrine which accurately describes the nature of modern British politics but which contributes nothing to the task of making British governments more accountable than they currently are. The result is not merely that there are whole areas of non-accountability (with the security services as the outstanding example), but that there is routinized non-accountability of a dominant executive cocooned in a culture of secrecy and protected against either serious legal challenge (despite the 'judge over your shoulders' warnings to civil servants in response to a more robust approach to judicial review)[10] or effective parliamentary challenge. It is doubtful that this makes for good government; it certainly does not make for good democracy.

Moreover, it is not just that the traditional doctrines of ministerial responsibility no longer correspond to contemporary political realities. More serious is the way in which these doctrines have been – and are still – regularly mobilized to block or curtail proposals aimed at enhancing the responsibility of the state to the people and their representatives. Thus the claim that the ventilation and redress of grievances is the function of the House of Commons in holding ministers to account could be used to obviate the need for other mechanisms (such as the Ombudsman, which in deference to traditional doctrine may still only be accessed through Members of Parliament) and is still used to deflect demands for a proper system of administrative justice. The doctrines are used to explain why civil servants can have no responsibility to a public interest (or even to a parliamentary interest) beyond their responsibility to ministers, and why Parliament and public can have no real access to the policy-making process. They are also used, of course, to show why proposals for a Bill of Rights would be quite inconsistent with the responsibility of ministers to Parliament.

Furthermore, major institutional innovations are introduced under the cover of doctrines which are already atrophied. Thus the most sweeping reorganization of the structure of government of recent years – the *Next Steps* programme of hiving off chunks of administration into free-standing agencies – was accompanied by charges that this process would entail a loss of accountability. It could be replied, quite properly, that it would entail nothing of the kind, since the new agencies would still be subject to ministerial responsibility to Parliament. The problem with such a reply is that it appeals to a doctrine which is itself in urgent need of challenge and change. The constitutionally orthodox is the politically bankrupt. A doctrine of ministerial responsibility which began life as an assertion of the democratic accountability of the executive has become the protective shield behind which governments can escape the rigours of effective democratic scrutiny and challenge.

The need, then, is for a contemporary theory and practice of responsibility. It is too important simply to be entrusted to the fictions of an inherited constitutional doctrine or the exigencies of an adversarial politics. The extended state of big government and quasi-government (and one of the paradoxes of privatization is that it extends the regulatory state rather than contracting it), with its intimate connections with the nexus of private governments, demands an equally extensive network of democratic accountability. This needs to be as varied, complex and extensive as government itself. It should supplement and nourish the political responsibility of adversarial party politics. It cannot be confined to Parliament; but Parliament can put it in place and watch over it. Meanwhile, the absence of effective and continuous accountability of this kind remains as damning testimony to a political tradition which has preferred not to take democracy with the seriousness it deserves.

8

Political culture: Democracy unvisited

> The main constraints upon government are cultural.
> Richard Rose *Politics in England Today* 3rd edition (1980)

When Dicey asked 'how far does a Constitution affect the character of a people?',[1] it was a question about the political culture. When Bryce described a 'democratic' person as 'a person of simple and friendly spirit and genial manners, "a good mixer", and who, whatever his wealth or status, makes no assumption of superiority',[2] it was an observation about the character of a democratic culture. Both agreed on the connection between a people and a politics. The nature of that connection, with its two-way flow between structures and attitudes, takes us inside a political system. In the case of Britain, what we find is a political culture in which democracy has been the uninvited guest rather than the active participant.

What we also find, though, is a political system in which the political culture has been endowed with a pivotal role. Precisely because the basis of the system was a flexible, informal, unwritten constitution, what was lacking in rules was claimed to be more than made up for by the character of the political culture. Indeed, rules were to be seen as a poor substitute for understandings. This line of argument has underpinned traditional accounts of British politics. It could be used (as it was by Dicey, at least in one mood) to celebrate a constitution of conventions as the sub-text of parliamentary sovereignty. It could also be used (and has been endlessly) to identify and explain the stability and continuity of British political arrangements, presented as the product of a cultural consensus on fundamentals. Generations of students have been invited to reflect on the eternal verities of Balfour's remark about the British people being 'so fundamentally at one that they can safely afford to bicker'.[3] That particular examination question will undoubtedly be another casualty of the Thatcher years.

What is significant, though, is that the consensus that was being claimed was not one which had been unduly disturbed by the arrival of democratic politics. The 'democracy' had not remade the polity in its own image, despite fears that it might, but rather the polity had incorporated and absorbed the democracy. In nineteenth-century terms, the problem to be overcome was that posed by an enlarged franchise. In twentieth-century terms, it was the entry into the system of a workers' party. When both were safely navigated, with the system intact, not only was there much relief, but also further inducement to pay tribute to a political culture which had made all this possible.

It was widely argued that the governing tradition of British politics, the transmuting of prerogative power into a dominant executive, was reflected in – and supported by – a congruent political culture. The British people liked 'strong' government, secure in the knowledge that their liberties were also secure. They also allegedly carried with them a considerable inheritance of deference, and this served both as a major support for a governing tradition and as a buffer against democratic excess. Deference has loomed large in accounts of British political attitudes and behaviour, whether in explaining the democratic fortunes of the Conservative Party or the survival qualities of the system as a whole. There is a certain irony in this attribution of the success of British democracy to the persistence and strength of pre-democratic dispositions, just as there is equivalent irony in its attribution to the politically skilful way in which the democratic impulse has been constrained and managed.

Not just irony, though; but also inaccuracy. For many years the reference point in these matters was the mid-century celebration of British 'civic culture' by American political science, with its identification of a benign mixture of citizenship and deference, activity and passivity.[4] This was still the reference point when, a quarter of a century later, it was announced with equal authority that the civic culture had collapsed under the weight of a populist kicking over of the traces of traditional authority.[5] Calmer heads have wanted to suggest a more subtle story, in which deference was never as significant as traditionally claimed and therefore its 'collapse' less apocalyptic. What is revealed instead is a widespread cynicism and distrust of politics and politicians, not as a new phenomenon, but already firmly in place when the civic culture was being celebrated, but now accompanied by a growing affirmation of the values of democratic participation.[6] The result is not a collapse of faith in democratic institutions, rather the reverse. What does result, though, is a challenge for a political system in which democracy has been sidestepped on the basis of an allegedly deferential culture and the needs of strong government.

In other words, the challenge in this case is to a particular political system which has taken some traditional pride in its ability to withstand the democratic current. In such a system it is not surprising if there develops a tension between what has been expected and what is now demanded, between old structures and new attitudes, or that there is a loss of trust associated with the gap between democratic promise and performance.[7] Nor is it surprising that this same system has experienced so much difficulty in constructing durable and successful policy instruments and institutions. It is not necessary to believe that the whole responsibility for British economic decline may be laid at the door of the political system to think that a system which has not taken seriously the task of developing a participatory policy style might have difficulty in securing consent and legitimacy for its activities. In such circumstances, strong governments can come to look very weak indeed.

A culture, and structure, for subjects will not serve well the needs of citizens. Yet in the politics of the extended state this comes to matter crucially, for it is necessary to persuade and engage citizens for the social and economic tasks that have to be undertaken. This requires a different kind of politics from what Marquand has called the 'club government' of Westminster and Whitehall,[8] which substitutes a private conversation for what should be a public dialogue, and shrinks democracy to a periodic engagement with the voters. Not only does that kind of politics lack its former cultural supports, but in modern conditions it is positively disabling. Yet it is remarkable how durable, and pervasive, adherence to it has been; and how, for a very long time, it could be cited as the benign secret of the British constitution.

It makes its appearance on all sides and in every way; it lies at the very core of the British political tradition. Its characteristics and consequences are all around us. It defines the texture of the system. From Bagehot through Orwell it has frequently been

writers and journalists who have best sniffed the air of British
politics and identified its authentic culture. Thus Hugo Young,
writing in the late 1980s, identified this democratic deficit:

> Contrary to popular myth, and to the incantations of political
> leaders who can hardly afford to give the question serious
> study, the British do not passionately care about democracy.
> As long as they get a vote every few years and the children
> don't starve, they are prepared to put up with almost anything
> politicians throw at them. They do not have the habit of
> making life difficult for government, especially a strong
> government. They are prepared to be quiet accessories to man-
> dates they never really gave. This preference, which is for
> strong government over accountable government, is to be
> found throughout the British parliamentary system.[9]

We might want to quarrel with the notion of 'preference' (which,
after all, is not the same as 'habit'), but there can be no serious
quarrel with the general judgement. Its truth is writ large over
the whole institutional landscape of British politics; and finds
its reflection in the conventional constitutional wisdom which
underpins that landscape.

It is to be seen in the dominance of the executive over the
legislature and in the dominance of the party machines over their
parliamentary flock. The requirements of democratic control and
scrutiny suffer routine relegation, not merely in Parliament but
throughout the system. Similarly, an unreformed electoral system
has found its traditional defence in an alleged antipathy on the
part of the British to 'weak' government. The system may not
be especially democratic (so this line of argument goes) but it
does at least (usually) deliver governments which can govern. If
we add on the notorious secrecy of British government – the
extent to which, in the words of a former Permanent Secretary,
'Whitehall's culture of secrecy is bred in the bone of British parliamentary democracy'[10] – the symmetry of the system is abundantly
clear. An élite political culture plays the game of club government,
with the associated fallout of leaks and spillages which passes for
public information; a popular political culture is distinguished by
(and celebrated for) its disposition to leave politics to the politicians; and the structural design of British political institutions,
of all kinds and at every level, suitably reflects and reinforces these
entrenched cultural characteristics.

It cannot be emphasized too much how central these matters
have been, and continue to be, to general explanations of British
politics. The consequences to which they give rise were identified
many years ago by R. H. S. Crossman:

> We are a nation deeply imbued with a sense of social status
> and inhibited by an oligarchic tradition, which makes responsi-
> bility the privilege of the educated minority, and irresponsi-
> bility the negative freedom of the half-educated masses. The
> leaders – and this applies at least as much in the Labour move-
> ment as outside it – profoundly distrust active democracy.[11]

But this was the voice of a political maverick, a radical who
wanted to disrupt the club and who knew what, at bottom, had
to be engaged with if this was to happen. The more familiar voice
has been the one finding in this same culture the reason why the
club has been in business for so long under the same management
despite all the changes outside – and wanting to affirm the considerable virtues of such continuity and stability. What this voice
has wanted to say, though perhaps not quite in this way, is that
a culture in which 'active democracy' was distrusted was not
merely a considerable resource but was essentially 'sound'. It did
not require elaborate machinery and formal rules to ensure that
honourable men did the decent thing, whether ruling or being
ruled.

This was why there was really nothing to worry about in a
political system of concentrated executive power without a formal
structure of checks and balances. At least, that was the traditional
claim. It was addressed, in particular, to the matter of parliamentary sovereignty. It might seem that a sovereign Parliament could
ride roughshod over the liberties of the people, but in practice, in
Britain, this was inconceivable. More precisely, it was culturally
inconceivable, for the political game was played by the rules by
people who had a shared commitment to liberty and a proper
respect for the wishes of the electorate. What was lacking in
formal constitutional accountability in the British system was thus
more than made up for in informal cultural accountability (and
without any debilitating loss of governing flexibility or strength).

It was in this confident spirit that, a generation ago, a distinguished constitutional lawyer felt able to point to 'the storm of
criticism which greets every extension of governmental power'[12]
as definitively reassuring evidence of the secure cultural roots of

British parliamentary democracy. A generation on, matters look rather different; so different, in fact, that much that has been taken on trust has to be questioned. It is not just that in the rough politics of the 1980s some of the traditional supports of responsible politics turned out to be conditional rather than permanent (as both effective oppositional politics and cabinet government collapsed), but that the cultural underpinnings of freedom and democracy turned out to be dangerously threadbare. Politicians not only hailed every new extension of governmental power as a gain for freedom, but called in aid a popular culture as a stick to beat those who were so clearly out of step with the times that they thought freedom meant something else. Thus Mrs Thatcher assured her television interviewer that ordinary people were 'much more in touch with security matters than people in the media.'[13] Far from providing a secure obstacle in the path of politicians who wanted to exploit to the full the opportunities for dominance offered by a malleable constitution, what the popular political culture provided was an open door.

The bluff had been called. It was quite possible for politicians not to play by the rules and to get away with it. Both civil liberties and constitutional proprieties turned out to be minority concerns, duly scoffed at by politicians who delighted in identifying their irrelevance to 'ordinary' people who displayed a proper disregard for such distractions from the real business of life. When the Major Government set about signalling its return to the ways of consensus and the rules of the game, this could not conceal the gaping hole that had opened up in the British political culture. The signal was that it was business as usual in governing Britain; the reality was that the old orthodoxies had visibly collapsed, but nothing had yet taken their place.

Thus observers have noted a weary cynicism about contemporary Britain, even that a whole 'culture of liberty'[14] was slipping away. Yet there was nothing surprising in the fact that a political culture which eschewed democratic citizenship should have acquired the habits of subjects. The only surprising thing was that such a culture should have been thought to provide a durable bulwark against executive tyranny or an effective substitute for constitutional guarantees. A ruling arrogance goes hand in hand with an indifferent people. Neither provides the basis for a mature democratic politics. This kind of politics has to be learned and constantly practised, in arguments, activities and institutions. Britain has had, and prided itself on having, a different kind of politics. Its consequences are all around us. It will not be changed by a quick constitutional fix. It would require nothing less that a *kulturkampf*. But perhaps that just restates the problem.

9

Democracy and ideology: The left

> The inevitable outcome of Democracy is the control by the people themselves . . .
>
> Sidney Webb *Fabian Essays* (1889)

It might be thought that the left would have been the natural leaders of a democratic *kulturkampf* in Britain. In part – and a substantial part – this had indeed been the case. It was from the left that the historic battle for universal suffrage was most energetically waged and it was on the left that the fruits of a democratic politics were most confidently expected. An enfranchised people would sweep away privilege and vote its way to socialism (or at least to the Labour Party's version of it). Indeed, this was precisely why those on the right got themselves into such a lather at the prospect of democracy and did their utmost to resist its progress. There might not seem to be a great deal more to be said about these ideological dispositions, beyond the fact that the expectations based upon them have been so comprehensively confounded.

Yet there is more to be said, certainly if the present democratic impasse is to be understood and negotiated. We need to know why there is a problem about democracy in Britain, despite the fact that it has had a powerful champion and carrier on the left. This suggests that we need to know not merely that the left has been in favour of democracy, but also what kind of democracy it has been in favour of (and against). What such an enquiry reveals is that, for good ideological reasons of its own, the left has been a willing accomplice in sustaining the traditional governing arrangements in Britain and resistant to the assorted demands for change. In pressing its own version of democracy, it has viewed the nature of the British political system more as opportunity than obstacle. Like much else in the Labour Party, this may now be changing (a consequence of its prolonged exclusion from power and its experience of the opportunities afforded by the political system to a different and uncongenial kind of ideological politics), but this merely points up the significance of traditional attitudes. One of the authors of the party's policy review in this area thought it would 'go a long way towards shedding the party's reputation for constitutional conservatism'.[1] On another view, though, what was proposed left that reputation firmly intact.

If we explore its basis, a number of strands emerge. At one level, Labour leaders have been under a standing obligation to affirm their constitutional respectability in response to the perennial Conservative allegation that the party was 'unsound on the constitution'. The fact that the charge was absurd did not remove its electoral or propagandist utility (though when Churchill tried during the 1945 election to conjure up the spectre of a *Gestapo* future under that pillar of propriety, Clement Attlee, the old electoral magic was asked to deliver more than even it could manage); nor did it remove the necessity for Labour leaders to emphasize the party's impeccable constitutional credentials and to repudiate any suggestion of dangerous constitutional radicalism. This obligation was not too onerous, since they believed it. Back in 1896 the Fabian Society had declared the British constitution to be 'a first-rate practical instrument of democratic government'[2] (certainly after the House of Lords was attended to) and generations of Labour orthodoxy were happy to agree.

There was a period, in the 1930s, when sections of the left persuaded themselves that a future Labour government would encounter such extra-constitutional obstruction that it would need to abridge normal constitutional procedures in order to carry through its programme. However, nothing more was heard of such matters when the post-war Labour government had no difficulty in carrying out its programme. As the historian of that government puts it, even the Lords 'took their medicine like sportsmen and gentlemen' and Labour reciprocated by displaying 'almost a reverence for the constitution'.[3] That reverence was most fully displayed when a leading member of that government, Herbert Morrison, subsequently wrote his *Government and Parliament* (1954) as an extended essay on the glories of the British constitution and its proximity to perfection. 'When the people cheer the Queen and sing her praises', he lyricized, 'they are also cheering our free democracy'.[4]

The seal was set, or so it seemed, on Labour's claim to parity of proprietorship of the British constitution. Moreover, in ideological terms, it could be seen as essentially congruent with the left's view of what democracy implied, notwithstanding its predemocratic antecedents and appurtenances. An enfranchized people could vote into power a party which could legislate in its interests and it was a cause for satisfaction, not regret, that a British government in command of the House of Commons had all the resources of a flexible constitution at its disposal. As G. D. H. Cole once put it:

> Our constitution is not based upon any fixed or immutable laws, nor do we require any special procedure to change it. This so-called flexibility is our greatest asset, it should enable the constitution to adapt itself momentarily to the desires and wishes of the people.[5]

The task was only to ensure that any remaining obstacles in the path of a popular majority were removed (with the House of Lords as the perennial focus), certainly not to invent new means – or sustain old ones – whereby governments were circumscribed in what they could do.

In other words, there was to the political left something particularly conducive to its ideology and purpose in the distinctive character of the British political system. If British socialism was about using the state to achieve social and economic objectives, then the British constitution seemed to put the state firmly at the disposal of majority parties. The left was instrumental in defining a twentieth-century theory and practice of the constitution that sustained this view, and in defending it against those who hankered after something else. It was the carrier of a collective and class view of representation as the appropriate form for the modern world – a view and a practice already rooted in Labour's trade union base – and refused to mourn with those who lamented a lost world of liberal individualism. It was the carrier of the associated drive towards party organization and disciplined party voting as the necessary reflection of a collectivist politics. It was suspicious of those who resisted the development of the flexible and discretionary administrative machinery required by an extended state. It was dismissive (notwithstanding earlier flirtations) of a whole range of proposals – whether to reform the electoral system or parliamentary procedures – which bore the stamp of individualist democracy and refused the logic of the collectivist state. In Ramsay MacDonald's words, such proposals were all to be seen as 'will-o'-the-wisps leading into bogs those who foolishly follow'.[6]

Thus Dicey may not have liked socialism, and collectivist critics have rounded on the ideological foundations of his account of the rule of law, but socialists have nevertheless liked Dicey's constitution. Its doctrine of sovereignty, once rooted in an enfranchised people, enabled a parliamentary majority to get its way. Its flexibility meant that the wishes of the people could be attended to without meeting structural obstacles. Its unitary character enabled a reforming government to bring its benefits uniformly across the land. It is scarcely surprising, then, that some of the most robust (and celebratory) accounts of British constitutional arrangements have come from the left, with antipathy reserved for those who sought to prevent a democratic constitution working as it should. Thus 'judicial review is the last doctrine that the Labour Party should champion' declared the *New Statesman* in 1955,[7] reflecting a view of judicial activism – seen again in the encounters between Labour governments and the courts in the 1970s – as a threat to the primacy of democratic politics.

In general terms, Harold Laski (whose reputation for a generation as Labour's leading constitutional theorist combined political radicalism with constitutional orthodoxy) argued that the British system offered 'the model upon which we can build the method of relationship between legislature and executive' for it enabled a government to 'drive its policy to the statute-book'.[8] Against this background, it is also not surprising that the revival of constitutional argument in the 1980s, with a government of the right vigorously deploying the resources of the constitution to drive its policies to the statute-book, should have elicited an uncertain response from an ideological tradition anchored in the view that the British constitution was congruent with its own version of democracy.

Or at least with part of it. For the left has also been attached to a more extensive and expansive understanding of the meaning and nature of democracy. Just as socialists were dissatisfied with liberalism's restricted conception of freedom and sought to socialize it, so too they have wanted to socialize democracy. It was not simply a matter of political citizenship, but also of social citizenship. A democracy was not merely a kind of political system, but a kind of society. As we saw earlier, this understanding of democracy has an impeccable historical pedigree (Aristotle, after all, was not a socialist) and the recent history of democracy is one of deliberate theoretical contraction and a reduction of its reach and ambition.[9] Aneurin Bevan was summoning up that older and larger tradition when, in 1940 with free Europe in retreat, he told the House of Commons that the 'sort of democracy' on offer before the war was not enough to rally the people of Europe against the dictators:

> If we are to persuade them, to enthuse them and inspire them with the defence of democracy, the conception of democracy has to be fitted into modern needs. We have to fill it up with a greater social content.[10]

However, not all the consequences of this mode of thinking have been fruitful. One consequence, as voiced by Sidney Webb, was the belief that there was a clear and uncomplicated road from political democracy to social democracy, that it was the function of the former to deliver the latter, and that the relationship between them was not an issue. A further consequence has been to focus the attention of the left on the extent to which a political democracy falls short of a social democracy, and the extent to which this shortfall is obfuscated by the prevailing ideology of (liberal) democracy. This is clearly an important and revealing enterprise in illuminating the nature of power behind the democratic and constitutional throne. J. A. G. Griffith has referred to this gap between the formal and the 'what actually happens' constitution and how:

> Time and again, it was usual to hear learned exposition about 'the theory of the constitution'. And occasionally when the lecturer had closed his bible it was possible to persuade him to speak a little about the reality of power in a capitalist parliamentary democracy.[11]

At times, though, in its endeavours to plug this gap, it has not always proved possible to persuade the left to think or speak seriously about political democracy itself.

Indeed, in some moods and at some times, the stance taken by sections of the left has revealed something more than neglect. The

Marxist and (erstwhile) fellow-travelling left, in particular, has been prone to write off 'bourgeois' (i.e. political, parliamentary) democracy as mere veneer and illusion, the mask behind which capitalism goes about its undemocratic business. This kind of devaluation in turn was sometimes used to sustain the claim that there was more 'real' democracy in countries without political freedoms but with socialist economies than in those countries where the reverse was the case. Even writers of progressive textbooks on the British constitution could tell their readers that 'the plain fact is that neither the word nor the concept of democracy helps us to choose between an egalitarian dictatorship and a system of representative government grounded in inequality'.[12] Of course all that was a long time ago. But old ideological habits die hard.

For a variety of reasons, then, and from a variety of perspectives, the left has had problems with democracy. When Roy Hattersley, then Labour's Deputy Leader, dismissed constitutional reformers as 'another brief outbreak of radical chic'[13] and defended the old orthodoxies, he had a long tradition behind him. It is a tradition in which a democratic collectivism is tied to a top-down constitution of a unitary state in which a strong single-party executive is born out of an electoral system which produces clear winners, a Parliament which registers what governments do and judges who know their place. In this way democracy functions as it should do, as the means whereby mandates are translated into governments without distraction, fragmentation or limitation. The people get their way. Political democracy is the route to social democracy. The trouble with this mode of thinking is not that it is wrong but that it is inadequate.

Its inadequacy has a number of aspects. It has, most urgently, made the left an accomplice in a political system which allows governments to do whatever, politically, they can get away with. What this means in practice has now been demonstrated by the Thatcher governments of the 1980s and, in the process, has provided the left with a painful constitutional education. Some on the left may still see it as a lesson for emulation; but more, it is to be hoped, will learn something else from the period. There is more to democracy than the winning of elections and more to governing in a democracy than getting your own way. The inadequacy of the left's traditional thinking on these matters is paralleled by the paucity of its past attention to issues of institutional design. In simplest terms, the left's attachment to democracy as a people's state has not been matched by an equivalent attention to how such a state should be run. Thus, the right found it alarmingly easy to launch a popular crusade against the state when the state hit the rocks in the 1970s, and the left found it alarmingly difficult to marshall a response.

It is too soon to judge whether the Labour Party, driven on by its freethinkers, will grasp the nettle of democracy. It could be its big idea, the basis for a programme of 'double democratization'[14] of polity and society rooted in the twin attachment to political and social citizenship. It could equally fall victim to the quick political fix or the belief that the next election, or the one after that, will put its traditional version of democracy back on course. It is always unwise to underestimate the conservatism of the British Labour movement, but it may just be that the need to find a new constituency in new times will turn out to have nourished a new democracy too.

10

Democracy and ideology: The right

> To place the chief power in the most ignorant classes is to place it in the hands of those who naturally care least for political liberty . . .
>
> W. H. Lecky *Democracy and Liberty* (1898)

The Conservative political tradition has always had a problem with democracy. Disliking it, as the threat posed by numbers to property, liberty and civilization, Conservatives have tried both resistance and domestication. It is all there in the history of late Victorian Conservatism, as political enfranchisement combined with a nascent socialism to frighten the life out of the defenders of the old order. A string of theorists and politicians – from Maine to Mallock, Salisbury to Lecky – worried away at the shape of things to come. A democratic collectivism seemed to be the order of the day, and Conservatives did not like it.

However, if the resistance option was forlorn, domestication was anything but. Always regarded as the Disraeli option, it eventually became the Salisbury option too (as even the old reactionary grasped the possibilities of a 'Villa Toryism'); and its fruits are to be seen in the political dominance of Conservatism over the century of universal suffrage. It is a story of extraordinary political success and adaptability, the more so for being to many of its own adherents so unexpected and unlikely. The Conservative acceptance of the new democratic order, signalled by its amenability to the 1918 electoral settlement around adult male suffrage, was undoubtedly hastened by the First World War as well as the demands of political survival in the conditions of mass politics. 'The war had turned "workers" into "soldiers" with incontestable claims to be considered "citizens" ', writes Peter Clarke: 'As the new armies grew, so did the Conservative conception of the electorate'.[1] Inevitably, it was not long before Conservatives had grafted the successful incorporation of democracy into their own celebratory accounts of the peculiar glories of the British constitution and of British history. It was yet another notch on the belt, one more vindication. Thus Enoch Powell could find an 'act of genius of the British people in the development of a feudal constitution into the modern British democracy',[2] with the representative system as the means by which this development was accomplished. Yesterday's threat had become today's achievement.

As with the left, though, what matters is what kind of democracy had been embraced. The short answer is that it was a Tory kind and, as such, essentially restricted. The Tory tradition is a governing tradition, not a tradition of the governed. It has combined an attachment to Tudor rigour with the balancing act of the Whig settlement. It stood for high politics against low politics, government from within against politics from without. It combined an affirmation of order and authority with respect to the national state with a proper regard for the legitimacy of Burke's 'little platoons' in civil society. It defended a view of representation that bestowed considerable autonomy upon the representatives and insulated them from excessive pressure from the represented. It emphasised the importance of leadership, and the importance of being led. It championed a mixed constitution (which it had once thought democracy would subvert by numbers), but one in which the governing function was clearly in the driving seat.

In all these respects Tory democracy defined itself as much by what it was against as by what it was for. The essence of the matter was famously expressed by Leo Amery in his *Thoughts on the Constitution* (1947), with its robust statement of a Tory view of the constitution as essentially top-down and executive-led and with the role of the electorate – and, indeed, of Members of Parliament – properly confined to merely approval or disapproval of the actions and proposals of governments. The peculiar appropriateness of the two-party system, its congruence with the British political tradition, was to be found in the primacy it gave to government and its translation of political choice into the simple categories of yes and no, for and against. In Amery's view, the liberals and radicals of the nineteenth century had 'grievously misled' people as far as these constitutional verities were concerned, crucially on the central truth that the British political tradition was one of 'government of the people, for the people, with, but not by, the people'.[3]

Tory democracy embraced popular government, but on condition that the people did not get in the way of the governing. The Tory appeal to the democratic electorate was that 'we shall rule, but in your interests', an effortless elision from a feudal to a democratic idiom. In party terms, the Conservatives sought to present themselves as the guardians of an ancient constitution against those who wanted to subvert its essential character and balance in pursuit of their ideological purposes. 'Conservatives believe in the Constitution as a safeguard of liberty', declared the party's manifesto for the 1950 general election: 'Socialists believe that it should be used for party ends'. The role of Labour's extra-parliamentary party was elevated by Conservative demonology to that of major constitutional threat, representing the twentieth-century version of 'pressure from without' against which the representative and governing function had to be protected, just as it had been against the radicals of the previous century. The way in which the Conservatives guaranteed such protection was there to be seen in the party's own internal organization, firmly asserting the leadership function, excluding the rank-and-file membership from any policy-making role and only recently finding (and losing) its leaders through the sordid business of election rather than the mysteries of emergence.

'We ought to understand it according to our measure; and to venerate where we are not able presently to understand.'[4] Burke's celebration of an ancient constitution, the custom and practice product of historical experience rather than of the infirmities of rational construction, was happily echoed by twentieth-century Conservatism, the more so when the democratic graft had been successfully made on to the old stock. Conservatives could take their stand on a traditional way of governing and take issue with those who could be presented as wanting to disturb and subvert it. For example, much political mileage over a long period was made out of the need to defend a territorial balance of power, in the interests of liberty, against the centralizing tendencies of Labour's social and economic programme. The party's 1955 election manifesto spoke of its commitment to 'cherish local democracy' and proudly boasted that 'so long as we are in office, there is no danger from proposals to strip local government of further powers'. In similar vein, R. A. Butler – one of the architects of post-war Conservatism – emphasized and extended this aspect of a balanced constitution and embrace of intermediate institutions as central to the constitutional outlook of Conservatives, so that in framing his 1944 Education Act he 'deliberately turned (his) back upon all suggestions that there should be nothing between the National State on the one side, and the individual on the other'.[5] Something has clearly changed in more recent times. But what – and why?

Here it is important to understand the twin-track character of the Conservative tradition, enabling it to switch track as circumstances demand (easily misinterpreted as a facility to stand on one's head) and not unconnected with its political success. One track emphasizes state, collectivity, order and authority; while the other track flies the flags of liberty, plurality and market. The Conservatism of little platoons is also the Conservatism of big battalions. When circumstances required, therefore, Conservatives were able to catch the collectivist tide, emphasizing that (unlike liberals) they had never had a problem about deploying the state for collective purposes. Had not Harold Macmillan once impishly remarked that Toryism was only a form of paternal socialism?[6] When circumstances changed, an alternative tradition could be summoned up to nourish the drive against collectivism and proclaim a market version of freedom. The consistent principle was to be in power.

It was when, in the 1970s, that Conservatives began to wonder whether they would ever be in power again, that there occurred a remarkable explosion of bile against the constitution of which they had long set themselves up as singular defender and interpreter. The traditional stance had been to guard the constitution against the legislative zeal of the Labour Party, but this was now replaced by a stance which made the constitution itself responsible for Labour's alleged legislative excesses. Lord Hailsham stands as the representative figure for this argument (although it was widely echoed and endorsed at the time), with his celebrated charge that Britain was 'moving more and more in the direction of an elective dictatorship' and that this was not a matter of transient political circumstances – which had merely exposed the underlying malady to view – but of a whole system of government where 'the political apparatus consists of an omnicompetent Parliament virtually consisting of a single chamber, dominated by a vastly powerful executive, and controlling a centralized bureaucracy, and completely uncontrolled by an effective judicial machinery'.[7] The remedy had to be as comprehensive as the disease: nothing less than a new constitutional settlement to institutionalize limited government.

The rest, as they say, is history. The Conservative administration elected in 1979, with Hailsham himself installed on the Woolsack, could presumably have embarked on a major programme of constitutional reform of the kind they had themselves recently recommended. It would have been a departure from a traditional Tory position on the constitution, in the direction of radical constitutional engineering and a liberal embrace of limited government, but the intellectual departure had already been made. Nor would it have been inconsistent with the economic liberalism which the Thatcherized party had now also embraced, for one strand of New Right thinking precisely identified the need for constitutional bulwarks to be established to prevent democratic governments doing the kind of things (like printing money) which they were inherently prone to do. Thus Hayek, widely regarded as a guru to the Thatcherite right, had not only disassociated himself from the Conservative tradition on the grounds that it was too much of a governing tradition, but had condemned the doctrine of unlimited parliamentary sovereignty as incompatible with constitutionalism and had sketched out a package of radical constitutional reforms designed to inhibit and constrain governments.[8] However, this was not an approach which commended itself to the Thatcher governments.

A cynic might say that elective dictatorship was only bad when the Conservatives were not getting elected and doing the dictating; and a cynic might be right. For it was not just that post-1979 Conservatism failed to act upon its own earlier constitutional analysis, but that it marched resolutely in the opposite direction. Before 1979 it had merely given us the theory of elective dictatorship; after 1979 it gave us the practice. Lord Hailsham had conjured up the spectre of a majoritarian tyranny which would:

> assert the right of a bare majority in a single chamber assembly, possibly elected on a first past the post basis, to assert its will over a whole people whatever that will may be . . . impose

uniformity on the whole nation . . . crush local autonomy . . .
dictate the structure, form and content of education.[9]

It would be difficult to find a more accurate prospectus for the
Thatcher years, as even the traditional and conventional inhibitions on British governments were casually and gleefully demol-
ished. In the name of 'democracy' (otherwise known as the ability
to win elections while the opposition was shooting itself in the
foot), here was a government which claimed the right to do
what it liked and was prepared to exploit to the full the ample
constitutional opportunities to do just that.

However, the necessary rhetoric of democracy concealed the
fact that it was precisely democracy which New Right doctrine
had identified as the difficulty to be overcome. As Andrew
Gamble says, in New Right discourse this was known as 'the
problem of democracy'.[10] It is the problem of big governments,
in the grip of big interests and big electoral pressures, taking
inflationary and interventionist options instead of adopting market
solutions. Democracy had to be tamed if the social democratic
state was to be rolled back. This was what led the New Right to
be interested in finding constitutional devices whereby democratic
governments could be held on the straight and narrow path of
market freedom. Perhaps this was a vain quest. Certainly, the
approaches canvassed revealed tremendous scope for ideological
disagreement about what was to be protected from what.[11] There
was anyway an inherent and intractable difficulty in seeking to
entrench the market against democracy in a democratic political
system which had been the means whereby market solutions had
themselves been challenged.

Whatever the reason, the Thatcher governments showed no
interest in constitutional engineering, certainly not to constrain
what governments could do. From within the resources of twin-
track Conservatism it was quite possible to be highly selective
about which bits of the state were to be rolled back and which
rolled forward, to fuse economic liberalism with a political Toryism in a combination greater than its parts. However, democracy
fared even less well in this new dispensation than in its traditional
Tory version. That traditional version had at least made its peace
with democracy and had accommodated it to its own governing
tradition, albeit in an attenuated form, while it managed to combine a firm grip on high politics by the central state with a positive

respect for the legitimacy of sub-state, voluntary and intermediate associations.[12] By contrast, the New Right approach was characterized by the identification of democracy as the key problem for the market order, the repository of demands which fed big government, requiring a response which hemmed in democratic governments and brought associations and interests to heel.

If the radical right government in Britain in the 1980s was not disposed to follow a course that might inhibit its own freedom of manoeuvre, it was more than disposed to use the exceptional opportunities afforded by a flexible constitution to press the rest of the New Right agenda. A key element in that agenda was a contraction of the arenas of democratic citizenship and an expansion of the arenas in which an individualized market order would operate. This was certainly one solution to the 'problem' of democracy. Whether it was any kind of solution to the problem of free and legitimate government in a modern extended state is another matter.

11

The missing traditions

> The central issue in British politics has not been how to curb the elective dictatorship but how to capture it.
>
> Dennis Kavanagh *Thatcherism and British Politics* (1990)

One conclusion is already clear. If a democratic deficit distinguishes British politics at the end of the twentieth century, an important part of the reason is to be found in the political traditions that have dominated British politics for much of the century. Ostensibly rivals, they have nevertheless colluded in the maintenance of a particular view of politics and of a system which gave expression to that view. The same point can be put in reverse: what has distinguished twentieth-century British politics has been the general absence of effective political traditions capable of pressing alternative definitions of a democratic polity. One such tradition is that of radicalism, or civic republicanism.

What kind of collusion has been engaged in? In a famous study, Samuel Beer pointed out that 'Socialist Democracy and Tory Democracy have a great deal in common' and that the outlook of both 'legitimizes a massive concentration of political power'.[1] A nineteenth-century liberal theory of the constitution (with its invocation of parliamentary sovereignty, ministerial accountability and the rule of law) might continue to be called in aid when appropriate constitutional rhetoric was required, but this could not for ever disguise the fact that the practice, and practitioners, of twentieth-century politics had a very different view of the organization of power and the proper conduct of politics.[2] This was a view which emphasized the requirements of strong party government and repudiated the inheritance of political individualism. Left and right might do so for different reasons, and for different purposes, but the effect was the same. A Tory governing tradition and a socialist collective tradition found common ground in applauding the merits of a top-down and flexible constitution and in resisting proposals which would imperil its unity, discipline and cohesion.

If we compare two post-war interpretations of the constitution from rival ideological traditions, the Tory version by Amery (1947) mentioned earlier and the socialist Laski's *Reflections on the Constitution* (1951), what is striking is not their differences (although the neo-Marxist Laski found some of the Tory Amery's institutional reform proposals a touch extreme), but their underlying agreement that the essence of the British system was to be found in a powerful executive and a two-party politics which clearly defined the tasks of governing and opposing. There should be no flirtation with any device which threatened this efficient secret of the system (such as proportional representation, judged by Laski to represent 'a continuous threat to the stability of executive power').[3] It was in these terms that the two-party system which dominated British politics for a post-war generation found its underpinning of constitutional interpretation.

The parties found the system to their ideological taste: the Conservatives because it was congruent with a Tory collectivism, Labour because it reflected a labourist and socialist view of class politics. Both agreed that there was no longer any place for a politics of antique liberal and radical provenance which sought to tie the hands of governors and governments. Elections were about finding governing majorities, not representing individual electors; and representatives were properly defined not by their membership of Parliament, but of parties. Far from being out of joint with the times, then, the character of the constitution was embraced by both major parties as peculiarly appropriate to the new dispensation. It might no longer correspond to traditional liberal theory, but so much the worse for the theory. The proper response was to revise the theory, not to seek to make institutional changes in a futile attempt to keep an obsolete theory intact.

This was a good point. The problem with the running liberal (also, usually, Liberal) lamentations about the divergence between the theory of parliamentary government and the practice of executive government was that they seemed rooted in the nineteenth-century world of limited government. Their grumbling ambition was not just to restore a constitution, but also a kind of society. The futility of the latter ambition nullified the former. Whereas the task was to develop political arrangements appropriate to the twentieth-century world of extended government, the liberal approach could too easily be seen as a vain attempt to revive institutional arrangements appropriate to the nineteenth-century world of restricted government. That said, though, and putting aside the element of self-interest involved in being a minority player in a system who wants to change the rules, the fact remains that it is largely from the liberal tradition that the issue of constitutionalism has been kept alive in twentieth-century Britain, even when times were bleak.

There was a period, early in this century, when there was a good deal of interest in the organization of extended government and how, in a variety of ways, a developing collectivism could be pluralized and democratized. Questions were asked, and variously answered, about new forms of both territorial and functional representation and about the taming of leviathan. For example, when the Webbs, archetypal state socialists, came to compose their socialist *Constitution* in 1920, an earlier satisfaction with the nature of British government had been replaced – under the influence of the new tendencies – by an indictment of the 'extraordinary hypertrophy of its political institutions'[4] and the need for extensive and elaborate reconstruction to meet the requirements of a modern democracy. The point about recalling this period (which effectively ended in the early 1920s) is not to reclaim specific proposals but to offer a reminder that there was a time when there was widely seen to be an issue needing attention. Equally, the point about identifying this dimension of the thinking of the majority ideological traditions which have dominated British politics from this period is because they have been united in not finding such an issue.

The system, as we have seen, was found to serve them well. Their competition was reserved for who should run it. When constitutional issues did rear their head – whether in proposals to strengthen parliamentary committees, reform the House of Lords, devolve powers from the centre, or join Europe – an alliance of left and right (or, in its personal appellation, during a crucial period, a Foot–Powell axis) could be relied upon to mount a concerted movement of resistance. More generally, constitutional issues were viewed as matters for containment rather than for exploration.

The essential task (with Scotland as the paradigm case in the

1970s) was to keep the lid on until things went off the boil. The containment became more difficult as the post-war political order broke down and a new kind of settlement was required. This was when, in the 1980s, the Conservatives no longer wanted to make the link between an executive-dominated constitution and a Tory collectivism, but now wanted to mobilize that constitution against collectivism of all kinds by means of a democratic by-pass operation. Labour, meanwhile, was thrown into some confusion by seeing the constitution it had espoused being used for purposes it loathed. Its eventual response was to embrace a number of specific reform proposals, but stopping short of a comprehensive critique,[5] sensing perhaps that the end of that road was not merely a new set of institutions but a new kind of politics. Whereas the Conservatives had used the constitution to address the 'problem of democracy' as their ideology defined it, Labour seemed to have a less sure conception of their own kind of democracy and, therefore, of its appropriate constitutional expression. As for the parties of the centre, the leading protagonists of wide-ranging constitutional reform during the 1980s, their proposals still suggested that they were addressing the problems of democratic governance of a complex modern state in terms of the institutional questions of a different era.[6]

This story has only to be told in outline for the character of British politics to be thrown into sharp relief, revealing both what is present and what is missing. It is not just that for much of this century the dominant forces in British political life, of both left and right, have sung the praises of a flexible polity (for as long, in fact, as they confidently expected to take regular turns in running it and enjoying its flexibility), but that their liking for it went beyond an expectation of proprietorship to include a symmetry with their general ideological outlooks and traditions. It was not always clear that this would be so. Indeed, much of the apprehension in governing circles about the advance of democracy was precisely because it threatened a fundamental reorientation of the polity. The Labour movement, in particular, was the carrier of a bottom-up democracy embedded in a dense network of self-governing associational life, such that 'nowhere could we find a more sturdy institutional protection for individuals against becoming a mass to be manipulated'.[7] Yet in its translation to the politics of the central state 'the movement which had invented the social forms of modern participatory democracy and practised them in

Union Branch and Co-op meeting, thereby laying a Tocquevillian foundation for democracy, was ironically fated to develop through its political party the threats of a bureaucratic state.'[8]

The real irony was that instead of using the state to extend its own practice of democratic citizenship, what Labour actually extended was the resources of a top-down constitution by supplying it with the armoury of mandates and manifestos to underpin a modern version of democratic party government. In drawing upon one part of its tradition, to sustain a politics of majoritarian collectivism, it not only neglected its other traditions, but eventually undermined them. When conjoined with a Tory tradition which pinned its hopes on democracy being contained, the character of modern British politics was effectively defined. It was a definition in which the state was there to be used, in a constitution which put it at the disposal of governments, with a belief in 'auto-limitation'[9] substituting for an effective system of checks and balances. It was also a definition in which politics was impoverished. In a winner-takes-all system, the only real competition is to be the winner. Citizens are reduced to voters, multiple arenas of citizenship narrowed to the periodic visit to the polling booth, professional party machines substituting for the authentic activity of democratic politics, a politics of observation rather than of engagement.

These issues are not unique to Britain. They are features of the organization of democracy in mass societies. Yet they have a particular form and force in Britain, simply because of the dominance of political traditions which – in the setting of a uniquely malleable constitution – have fostered rather than mitigated them. These are traditions which have emphasized the winning and using of power, but have neglected the sharing and curbing of power. That is why they have traditionally found the nature of the British constitution very much to their taste. What has been missing, but may now be taking shape, is an attention to those other traditions – of pluralism, participatory citizenship and constitutionalism – which have been the dogs that did not bark in twentieth-century British politics. Yet these are the ingredients for a civic republicanism which, when all else has failed, may offer a basis for legitimate rule in complex and difficult times.

If so, a dollop of radicalism will be required. Not the radicalism (of the kind Mrs Thatcher liked to profess) which involves doing whatever comes into your head, and taking full advantage of a system which enables you to do just that, but the radicalism which involves keeping a close watch and a tight hold on power and the powerful. It means rules and rights, a procedural framework within which the substantive business of politics has to be conducted. In contrast to that high-minded version of citizenship in which rulers act in the public interest and the governed perform their proper civic duties, radicalism does not take power on trust. It is a sordid tradition which asks the dirty questions. As such, it is indispensable. The absence of a radical tradition of this kind in recent British politics – the obverse of the dominance of traditions which, for their own reasons, have wanted to keep governments strong and constitutionally unencumbered – is apparent on all sides.

It is apparent, to take just one kind of example, in the routine patronage – of office and reward – which is ladled out without democratic scrutiny or control in Britain. The ministerial payroll of placemen has expanded as parliamentary independence has contracted. Cabinet ministers slip easily, too easily, from ministerial office to the boardrooms of the privatized corporations they were responsible for establishing and regulating. The Thatcher years saw a ruthless deployment of patronage to reward those who were 'one of us', including those businessmen who had shown their devotion by making lavish contributions to Conservative coffers.[10] Members of Parliament have increasingly come to regard membership of the House of Commons as offering lucrative opportunities for extramural employment, with two out of three MPs now in other paid work and nearly one in three acting as a paid parliamentary consultant.[11] Public bodies of all kinds have been stuffed full of compliant ministerial appointees. 'Not, perhaps, since the eighteenth century', writes John Grigg, 'has government maintained itself so shamelessly by the exercise of patronage.'[12]

Equally, it was not for nothing that the radicals of the eighteenth century waged war on a politics of patronage. It was an index of the corruption of government. It remains so today. The fact that it is alive and well in the democratic age of big government is further testimony to the way in which, in Britain, a traditional politics of understandings has not been constitutionalized. In turn, this reflects the 'progressive dilemma'[13] of twentieth-century British politics, the failure to construct a progressive and radical coalition capable of challenging both old Labourism and old (and new) Toryism in the name of democratic citizenship. This, too, is a missing tradition and a reminder that ideas, including ideas about governing, need their carrier.

12

Centralism and localism

The . . . assault on local accountability, indeed on democratic pluralism in Britain, was the sorriest chapter of the Thatcher era.

The Times, 25 January 1991

If we want further evidence of the dominant traditions – and missing traditions – of modern British politics, it is only necessary to look at territorial politics. Similarly, any reconstruction of the basis of the British political system would have to include the division of power by area. The whole issue of territorial democracy is acute, protracted and unresolved. It makes its presence felt on many sides – on Europe, on Scotland, on local government – and meets a political tradition both unprepared and unwilling to take it seriously. It is a political tradition in the grip of an ideology of centralism, but increasingly overwhelmed by the issues with which it is called upon to deal.

On Europe, for example, it was revealing that the response of the British government to the prospect of closer political union was to say that it neither liked nor understood the word 'federal' and wanted nothing to do with it, calling in aid both assorted dictionaries and our old friend the sovereignty of Parliament.[1] It might have been supposed that the government of a United Kingdom would have something to contribute to a European discussion of a multi-national territorial polity, but not so. Instead, the most centralized state in the European Community could offer only ritual denunciations of an alleged European centralism.

What was missing was any sense that power could be shared and redistributed between states and within states, upwards and downwards, with democratic structures to match, in a complex and variegated pattern appropriate to tasks, demands and needs. Yet this was a depressingly authentic response on the part of a political tradition that had resolutely avoided thinking about power in this way.

The same avoidance was apparent in the centralist assault on local government which distinguished the Thatcher era. The nature of that assault is amply documented and requires no further recitation here.[2] It is difficult to decide which is more depressing – the fact of the demolition job on local government or the further fact that it was undertaken so wantonly, without any clearly articulated justification in the ideology of a unitary state. It was driven by a Treasury desire to control local spending and a political animus against ideologically unpalatable local councils, but key issues of territorial politics which should have been raised were simply ignored. The fact that traditional accounts of centre–local relations were being subverted (ones, moreover, which had figured prominently in traditional Conservative accounts of these relations) was not allowed to distract attention from the matters in hand. Truly here was a practice without a theory. The battering ram of parliamentary sovereignty was deployed to knock down one version of centre–local relations, but without either a developed alternative offered in justification or even a recognition that fundamental questions of territorial politics were necessarily being raised.

These questions, though, were not simply those turning on the rival legitimacies of Westminster and local democracy. It is certainly the case that the way in which Westminster democracy stamped on local democracy fuelled doubts about its own democratic legitimacy, as well as providing a ruthless constitutional education; but that response which simply equated the object of attack – the existing form of local government – with something to be described as 'local democracy' was nevertheless wide of the mark. What was missing was the recognition that *both* the existing Westminster and local versions of democracy were properly in question, and not merely the relation between them. Back in 1967, the Maud Committee (on the management of local government) put the point bluntly:

We have found no evidence to support the belief that our local government has some uniquely democratic content. Whether the test is public interest, as exemplified by the percentage poll at elections, or the extent to which members of the public, individually and in their associations, are drawn into its processes, our local government does not appear to be especially democratic.[3]

It is not useful to confuse the idea of local democracy with its existing form and structure.

Indeed, the trend seems to be for local government increasingly to replicate the politics of Westminster government rather than to provide an alternative version of democratic politics (although a new trend of enforced power-sharing in county government was the most interesting result of the 1993 local elections). The story is one of ever tighter party control and of decisions taken behind closed doors in ruling group meetings, with meetings attended by the public becoming increasingly meaningless in terms of real debate and decision.[4] Officers are ever more politicized, while ruling groups are disposed to use their power of patronage and appointment (as with the appointment of school governors) to fix the system in their own image. In all of this the impression is of a local government trying to emulate Westminster rather than to provide a democratic antidote to it. If those attacking local government during the 1980s were careless of the idea of local democracy, some at least of those defending local government were no less careless in making it synonymous with local democracy. The democratic tests – of accountability, representation, participation and openness – apply across the board.

But the idea matters. These tests are more easily met if power is diffused and pluralized. Yet Britain presents the case of a political system which is exceptionally centralized and concentrated. While the trend in other European democracies is towards greater deconcentration – with some evidence that regionalization may also be a motor of economic advance – the trend in Britain has been resolutely in the opposite direction.[5] What we are dealing with is British exceptionalism. Where others have great provincial capitals, we have London government. Where others have taken the division of power by area seriously, even constitutionally, we have sought to avoid the issue if at all possible or to convert it into a task for political management when necessary. This was not always so – in the early part of this century there was a good deal of discussion about territorial politics, especially on the left, as part of a wider discussion about the shape of the collectivist state[6] – but it has been so for much of this century and, in significant respects, for much longer.

What has to be understood (and addressed) is a theory and practice of centralism. On one side it is a story of the English centre engaged upon an enterprise of territorial management in relation to its peripheral nations, an enterprise that seemed to have been concluded by the early 1920s with the Irish settlement, but in reality was not. What also seemed to have been established from the same period (and for half a century plausibly was) were the terms of the relationship between central and local government. Here the story is of a London centre operating a doctrine of separate spheres in its relations with the localities, producing a 'dual polity' in which high politics was the secure preserve of the centre with low politics remaining for the localities.[7] This arrangement was underpinned by a common culture in which both sides accepted this division of labour and was reflected in a pattern of political life in which there was remarkably little interpenetration of local and national élites.

It was also underpinned by a common ideology of centralism on the part of the key actors in British politics. A Tory preoccupation with the integrity of high politics and the territorial management of the union was matched by Labour's preoccupation with universalizing its class project through the capture and deployment of the resources of the central state. The case of Labour is particularly interesting, because it was not always so clear that its role would come to be described in quite this way. For what happened was that a party of the periphery – with extra-parliamentary roots and demands for home rule all round – became a party of the centre. In doing so it played an important role in sustaining and strengthening the British central state in the twentieth century.[8] More generally, this can be seen as one essential element in the process whereby a series of critical challenges to the strategy of territorial management early in this century were resolved in a manner which kept a traditional territorial politics intact. As Bulpitt puts it:

> It had been a close run thing, but the eventual outcome was a United Kingdom dominated by territorial conservatives: a strange alliance of Ulster Unionism, the Labour Party and the Conservative Party now operated. The period of potential upheaval was over.[9]

It was only over for a time, though a rather long time (stretching from the 1920s to the 1970s). It was during this time that a familiar portrait and interpretation of the British polity gained wide currency, with a secure place within it for the territorial distribution of power. Indeed, this security could be cited as evidence of the deep roots of Britain's informal constitution. While less fortunate countries were obliged to pursue democratic pluralism through constitutional engineering, in Britain it was firmly anchored in a political culture which guaranteed the integrity of a dual polity. The existence of such a solid guarantee, widely celebrated in descriptions of the system and with political competition for the place of chief guarantor, could in turn be cited as compelling evidence that Britain enjoyed a kind of territorial pluralism which was more than a match for more formal arrangements elsewhere.

It was usually described in the language of 'partnership'. This was fine for as long as the partners played by the rules of the game of separate spheres, which from the 1970s they ceased to do. Even while they did, though, there was an inherent contradiction waiting in the wings. It was the contradiction between 'partnership' and 'sovereignty', between a culture and practice of power-sharing and an axial principle of primacy and dominance. These were ultimately incompatible, notwithstanding the fact that they managed to live together for a long time. When the breakdown came, all the unresolved questions of boundaries and legitimacies were exposed. They were speedily, if bloodily, resolved by the hammer blow of 'sovereignty', but such a resolution was achieved at an exceptionally high price. Not merely was the contradiction within the territorial polity opened to view, but there was a gaping hole in the tapestry of the constitution formerly occupied by a traditional account of the division of power by area.

The breakdown of the territorial polity in the 1970s and 1980s had many aspects and sources. The striking and common feature, though, was the sheer unpreparedness of the political culture to make a coherent and positive response. Nowhere was this more so than with the issue of Scottish and Welsh devolution, where majority opinion in both main parties seemed only to want this irritant in the system to go away and could translate this only into a botched politics of containment. There was neither a principled affirmation of the union nor an imaginative grasping of the opportunities for devolved power in an over-centralized state (and including England too).[10] In similar fashion, the local government battles of the 1980s were waged in a context where there was little recognition of the actual nature of sub-national government and an absence of any reasoned philosophy in relation to it.[11] An old conception had clearly broken down, but there was a resolute disinclination to explore new conceptual territory. How much better to pretend that nothing much had happened, a pretence that could be augmented by a bit more ad-hocery. In this sense it was entirely characteristic that a new reorganization of local government should have been initiated in 1991 only as a by-product of the need to do a political fix on the poll tax.

Yet containment made sense if the intention was to prevent fundamental questions about the political system from emerging. For the point about the issues of territorial politics was precisely that they did, if not strictly demarcated and domesticated, weave together into larger and systemic questions. They forced the matter of sovereignty into view. They probed ideological assumptions. They required powers and competencies to be clarified, written down and adjudicated. They asked about the appropriate organization of democracy. They defined identities. A political system, and political traditions, which had preferred to avoid such questions – or had wanted to regard them as safely settled – were understandably disposed to seal off issues which necessarily raised them. In part, at least, this was a matter of not knowing quite what to do about them. The problem with this response is that it is no longer available.

It is no longer available because one version of the territorial polity has broken down, but nothing has taken its place. It has broken down both in relation to the constituent nations of the United Kingdom and in relation to the balance between central and local government. There was no final territorial settlement by the 1920s, although there seemed to be, and there was no permanent containment achieved in the 1970s. The territorial polity is in tatters. It is immobilized by developments in Europe. It can only observe the confident constitutional claims from Scotland. There is a hole where local democracy should be. The need for a new territorial settlement is matched only by the general unwillingness and incapacity to devise one.

It is not just that there is an inappropriate structure of centralism, but that it is rooted in an obsolete ideology of centralism. This makes change and adaptation peculiarly difficult. A unitary dogma of sovereignty, traditionally buttressed by the ideological dispositions of the main twentieth-century political traditions, has blocked the path to secure forms of shared and devolved power. Yet it is precisely this which is needed and demanded. A centralized state sinking under the weight of burdens it cannot carry meets the requirements neither of efficiency nor democracy. It seems likely, and desirable, that the pattern of government in the future will be a matter of different levels with different functions, from the global and European to the regional and intensely local. This requires both a new institutional imagination and a new democratic imagination. The tragedy is that in Britain a doctrine of sovereignty limits the imagination to the national state and imposes the curse of centralism on the theory and practice of the organization of power.

13

Consumers, producers and citizens

> In the early stages of this controversy each of the parties tended
> to state its position in the most extreme form; and to claim in
> fact that the only genuine Democracy was one that accepted,
> exclusively, the basis of Man as Producer, or Man as Con-
> sumer, or Man as Citizen, respectively.
>
> Sidney and Beatrice Webb *A Constitution for the Socialist Com-
> monwealth of Great Britain* (1920)

In the early part of this century there was not only a good deal
of interest in the division of power by area, but also in the division
of power by function. Issues of territorial democracy were conjoined with issues of functional democracy. There was widespread
resistance, amongst political intellectuals of assorted persuasions,
to the claims of a 'sovereignty' which demanded a one-dimen-
sional obligation and identification with the central state; and an
affirmation of a plurality of identities and allegiances which
implied what the Webbs (hardly pluralist zealots) described as
the 'manifold' organization of democracy.[1] There was room for
considerable disagreement about both the importance to be
attached to the different functions (notably those of consuming,
producing, and being a citizen) and their structural consequences;
but the recognition of plurality – and of manifoldness – was shared
ground.

The point of recalling this period is not to make it available for
easy borrowing (there is much that could be usefully borrowed,
but also much that is time-expired), but to provide a reference
for subsequent developments and current dilemmas. In brief, the
insights of that earlier period were aborted rather than developed,
with consequences of direct relevance to contemporary discon-

tents. In some ways there is a parallel with the story of the territorial polity. Just as the culture of separate spheres left high politics and sovereignty intact, with key issues of territorial politics avoided over a long period; so too a culture of creeping corporatism combined with formal obeisance towards the boundary lines of state and civil society and adherence to conventional constitutional wisdom to sustain the view that it was possible to have a practice without a theory and that questions about the nature and purpose of any new institutional order could safely be ignored. As with the territorial polity, a cultural kicking over of the traces has exposed the limitations of an old order (certainly in terms of any secure institutional pluralism), but without providing a satisfactory basis for a new one.

Here, too, there was an inherent contradiction between a pluralist power-sharing (functional now, not territorial) and a doctrine of parliamentary sovereignty. From early in the century the major corporate institutions of business and labour began to share in the running of the state 'in ways not dreamt of when Dicey in the late nineteenth century canonised the doctrine of parliamentary sovereignty'.[2] However, instead of such developments providing the opportunity both for radical institutional remodelling and for doctrinal revision, the pretence was sustained that nothing very significant was happening. Thus Britain has a long history of corporatist practices and initiatives – from the Whitley Joint Industrial Councils of the First World War and the National Industrial Conference of 1919, right through to the National Economic Development Council of the 1960s and Social Contract of the 1970s – but this has not been accompanied by equivalent constitutional engineering. A whole raft of suggestions (including those for industrial parliaments and functional assemblies) surfaced at different times and from different quarters, but were not taken up. Thus the particular initiatives which could have provided the basis for a continuous and coherent practice failed to do so and were easily aborted by Thatcherism after 1979 (and by post-Thatcherism, as with the abolition of the NEDC in 1992). As with territorial politics, the contradiction was resolved in favour of – and by – sovereignty.

However, the price was high, and anyway all was not quite as it seemed. The price to be paid was in terms of the lack of purposive machinery required to drive a modern democratic state and its economy. 'Again and again', writes David Marquand, 'would-be interventionists were frustrated by the lack of a tradition of developmental intervention, and by the widespread belief that such intervention was either impossible or undesirable.'[3] Labourism and neo-liberalism combined to sustain this belief. Thatcherism was therefore kicking at an open door. Under the cloak of parliamentary sovereignty an informal system of collaborative government of the extended state had necessarily come into being, but it had never been formalized in constitutional terms and lacked the underpinning of political traditions which might have accomplished this. It was not difficult, therefore, to sweep away what, in a sense, had not existed. However, under the cloak of sweeping it away the fact of extended government remained, with a dense network of collaborative and regulatory arrangements and massive interpenetration of public and private power.[4] In significant respects the 'rolling back of the state' intensified rather than diminished such interpenetration.

The real effect of Thatcherism was to keep the door firmly closed on the system of informal power and on any attempt to constitutionalize it. The doctrine of parliamentary sovereignty provided, as ever, the means and the justification. This process was helped by the fact that the dragon to be slain ('corporatism') had few friends and many enemies. Both left and right queued up to denounce it and to disassociate themselves from it, confirming the common ground and shared antipathies of political traditions. What was missing was a recognition that an open and explicit corporatism (which, of course, was not what had been developed) provided a means whereby the major collaborative social interests were identified, articulated and made visible, and extended government brought under the umbrella of the constitution with an enhanced accountability.[5] As such it involved a break with 'sovereignty' and a formalization of an institutional pluralism embracing producer, consumer and other interests. It was characteristic that such a challenge to a traditional way of ruling – and to a traditional doctrine about ruling – should have encountered widespread resistance from political traditions which had long avoided the task of bridging the gap between a doctrine of governing and a practice of governing.

Nor was this the only respect in which there was a failure to explore the implications for democracy of a plurality of roles and identities (which could not properly be swept up together in a single mode of representation or single dimension of citizenship).

Citizenship is many-sided because citizens are; and because power has more than one face. It does make sense to speak of social and economic citizenship and to seek to give content to the rights (and responsibilities) attaching to such citizenship. Again, in Britain, this has been informal and implied rather than explicit and declaratory. It was implied in the post-war settlement of the late 1940s and implicitly unpicked in the dismantling of that settlement in the 1980s. It has been possible both to expand and contract – indeed, to redefine – the social and economic basis of citizenship without any formal engagement with the issue. This is an unsatisfactory, if characteristic, situation and it remains central to the larger task of giving meaning, content and status to democratic citizenship.[6]

Still with that early century reference point, there has also been a retreat from even the most tentative attempts to explore issues of workplace democracy. The position of the producer was once central to discussions of the shape and nature of a pluralized democracy, so much so that there were those who wished to reconstruct the polity on the basis of producer democracy – and who won widespread support for this proposition, at least for a period.[7] However, even in its more sedate form of 'industrial democracy' it has been difficult to graft this extended understanding of democracy onto existing British stock (as evidenced both by the fate of the Bullock proposals in the 1970s – flawed though these proposals were – and by the stance of the British Government a decade later in resisting a Europeanization of workers' rights, including participatory rights). Yet the issue remains and intensifies, as the best of the neo-pluralist theorists of democracy have acknowledged and addressed. There *is* an issue about the 'private' power of the corporation in a democracy and about the legitimate stakeholders in that private power. As Robert Dahl has famously argued, 'a system of government Americans view as intolerable in governing the state has come to be accepted as desirable in governing large economic enterprises.'[8] Both producers and consumers (and not just shareholders) have legitimate rights in relation to such 'private' power, and a democratic polity will seek to give effect to them. There will be no uniform method or structure whereby this is done (a central defect of the Bullock approach was to embrace a single-channel formula), but nor need there be. A certain untidiness is the hallmark of a vigorous pluralist democracy.

Nor is there any reason why such developments should stop at the private sector. One of the signal if unintended services performed by the privatization programme of the 1980s was to demonstrate that a robust irreverence was the proper stance to be adopted in relation to the traditionally demarcated boundary lines of the 'public' and the 'private' (at least in relation to the organization of power). It was necessary to think freshly about what it meant to have public services in the private sector. Privatization came from the political right; but need not end there,[9] and it fed back into the private sector itself in terms of the issues it raised. Equally, the kind of arguments traditionally advanced (electoral representation, parliamentary sovereignty) for the way in which public services were – and were not – organized have also been called into question. There is no reason, for example, why forms of 'service democracy' should not be developed in the public sector any less than forms of 'industrial democracy' in the private sector. The same considerations apply to both.

However, this is not the same as saying that there is no distinction between the public and the private, only that old boundary lines and old arguments have to be recast. In fact, the task is precisely to try to define what is distinctive about the public sphere and what this means for the organization and delivery of public services. This is directly relevant to – because it was what was largely missing from – the debate on public services which has been a significant feature of recent British politics (and which was given another official twist by the glossy launch of a Citizen's Charter for public services in July 1991 by the Conservatives, following on the heels of similar 'charters' from the opposition parties.[10]). The wag who remarked that the trouble with these public service charters was that, like the buses, you did not see any for a long time then several came along altogether had got a good point. They had not come along for a number of important reasons, not the least of which was that constitutional orthodoxy maintained that issues of accountability and redress in relation to the operation of government were securely and satisfactorily handled by a sovereign Parliament. This has been a powerful fiction over a long period, blocking a whole raft of developments and at great cost to the consumers of government.

It was further buttressed in the case of the Labour Party – the traditional party of the public services – by a top-down approach to service delivery and by an institutional attachment to producer groups which made it difficult also to be the champion of the service users. When the Thatcher Government launched its assault on the public services, on the basis of a 'private good, public bad' credo which sought to remodel public services by introducing private sector practices (and encouraging opportunities to exit altogether), Labour's initial response confused a defence of the principle of public services with a defence of existing modes of organization and delivery. Over time, though, it recognized that public services would only be defended and valued if they were much more user-focused than in the past.[11] When the Major Government also decided to fly the flag of public service consumerism, it seemed that everyone was now telling the same story.

This was not the case, but could easily seem so. At the heart of the confusion was an unwarranted running together of consumers and citizens (one good reason for preferring the term 'user' to 'consumer' in the context of public services is precisely because it sits more easily alongside a wider citizenship). It is not just that consumers and citizens are not the same, but that they are fundamentally and intrinsically different. Rudolf Klein, writing about the 'conceptual muddle' on these issues in the context of the National Health Service, makes the point well:

> Participation is about politics: the involvement of citizens in the process of making decisions on issues of public policy. The point is obvious enough, yet all too often forgotten in the debate about participation. For when we examine the arguments for more participation we frequently find these being put in terms of giving more power to the consumer. Yet the difference between citizens and consumers is all important.[12]

It is not just immediate consumers who have an interest in services, while consumer and citizen interests may conflict. Moreover 'the language of consumerism is that of the economic market place rather than that of the political market place',[13] the language of individuals getting what they want not the language of equity and the collective interest. In many public services (with health and education as the outstanding examples) the application of a pure consumerist model – of the kind foreshadowed in the legislation of the 1980s – would directly subvert the non-market and non-individualist basis upon which such services were organized and which defined their 'public' character.

This is why it is mistaken to dismiss the outbreak of public service consumerism on the part of the Conservative Party and the neo-liberal right as mere political gimmickry. Its significance is precisely that it seeks to substitute a consumer democracy for a citizen democracy. Thus a charter for consumers is described as a charter for citizens (though its supervising minister, William Waldegrave, conceding its absence of substantive citizen rights, has even said that it should perhaps really have been described as a charter for managers). We have a citizen's charter, but not a citizens' charter; and the apostrophe matters. A polity in which there is an urgent and overdue need to extend democracy is offered instead its further contraction. There is a world of difference between an approach to public services that seeks to empower users as citizens (and which puts issues of redress and choice alongside issues of accountability and representation) and an approach that turns public users into private consumers. Similarly, there is a gulf between the development of a 'public sector pluralism'[14] rooted in an expanded sense of the organizational possibilities of a pluralist democracy which takes account of consumer, provider and community needs and a fragmentation of the public sector into a set of private interests. At the beginning of this century it was widely argued that democracy should be extended to embrace Man as Producer. It is significant that at the end of the century what is on offer is Man as Consumer, but not now as an extension of democracy, rather as its privatized substitute.

14

Reconstructions I: Representation

> The claims of *parliaments* to monopolize and exhaust the representative process – on which their theory still depends – are in actual conditions unrealizable.
>
> Raymond Williams *Democracy and Parliament* (1982)

There is no doubt that 'representation' is 'one of the slippery core concepts of political theory'.[1] There is equally no doubt that the British political tradition, at least in recent times, has shown little interest in trying to get a reasonably secure grip on it, nor that any democratic reconstruction of the British polity would need to have a revised view of representation as one of its basic ingredients. Whether we understand the term as meaning 'microcosm' (an accurate reflection of the represented) or as 'principal-agent' (acting on behalf of),[2] with all the modulations of each, the British representative system is in an unreconstructed mess.

It is not necessary to believe in the chimera of perfect representation to take the view that the British system exhibits a remarkable propensity both to be unreflective of the larger society and to avoid acting on its behalf. It sustains itself with a whole series of fictions and elisions. A Member of Parliament claims with marvellous effrontery to represent constituents a majority of whom almost certainly voted for someone else. One House of Parliament claims a representative status (even sometimes claims a representative superiority) notwithstanding the fact that its members have not been voted for at all by anybody. Parliamentary majorities claim to represent 'the people' on the basis of an electoral 'mandate' to govern in a particular way, despite the fact that the people in question were a minority of those voting (and an even smaller minority of those entitled to vote) and that, in policy terms, it is impossible to know what has been voted for and what against. A legislative assembly claims to be 'representative' even though whole sections of the represented (in age, class, gender and ethnic terms) are hardly represented at all and the assembly itself is still so organized as to be incompatible with normal family life.

These familiar observations on convenient fictions serve as a reminder both of the potency and the elusiveness surrounding the matter of representation. Potent because here is the axial legitimating principle of modern democratic politics, the foundation of the claim to rule; and elusive because its meanings are effortlessly blurred, merged and exchanged before they can be pinned down and put into service. There is, of course, something inherently second hand and unsatisfactory about the idea of representation, at least to zealous democrats, an acknowledgement that this division of labour in the business of ruling is the best that large societies can do. An associated dissatisfaction necessarily attaches to the practice of representation, simply because of the manifold difficulties involved in achieving a correspondence – on a range of fronts – between those who represent and those who are represented. It is relatively easy, for example, especially for those with a predilection for treating the study of politics as a branch of mathematics or economics, to demonstrate the inability of electoral systems of any workable kind to produce genuinely representative outcomes. We simply have to do the best we can, taking a range of relevant considerations into account.

However, this rather unheroic conclusion should not be allowed to obscure the fact that it is upon the representative principle that modern societies have pinned their democratic hopes. 'Borrowing Bagehot's metaphor', writes Carol Harlow, 'we might describe representation as the buckle between power and people.'[3] So it matters; and doing the best we can, getting the right adjustment on the buckle, becomes more important than it sounds. The fact is that we are not doing the best we can; and it will take more than a fix of the electoral system (important and necessary though that is, in view of how the present system now operates) to get the ship of state on to a better course. The basic problem is that 'representative government' has been made to seem easier than it should have been. Just as representative government (of a kind) existed before electoral democracy, so representative government with electoral democracy does not exhaust the range of representative possibilities available to, and required by, the democratic governance of modern states.

In Britain, in particular, we have been too ready for too long to swallow Dicey's account of how a sovereign Parliament necessarily became the agency of a sovereign people through the institution of electoral democracy. It would have been sensible, not least because of those peculiarities of the British system of government which actually translated a sovereign Parliament into a sovereign executive, to pay more attention to those who wanted to suggest some of the other consequences of mechanisms which allowed rulers to ground their claim to rule in the fact that they were the elected representatives of a sovereign people. This is the extent to which 'the dominant idiom – representative democracy as democracy – in fact serves to legitimate modern big government and to restrain it hardly at all'.[4] Indeed, it can be mobilized against other modes of representation and other forms of democracy (as it was ruthlessly during the 1980s, but is routinely at other times too).

Elections are important. They are a blunt, indispensable instrument for putting rulers in and kicking rulers out, but they are useful for rulers too. If they become too blunt (for example, in the relationship between votes and outcomes) then there may well be an associated loss of legitimacy, which has increasingly become the case in Britain and provides the best reason for thinking that a shift from a simple plurality system of voting to one with a greater element of proportionality will eventually be necessary (and not just desirable). It is worth recording again that no British government since 1935 has been returned with a majority vote. However, it is misleading to reduce the matter of representation to the issue of the least imperfect system of voting. That reduction is precisely the problem, or at least one of a related cluster of problems. Instead of regarding electoral democracy (in whatever structural form) as the unproblematical and exhaustive basis of representative government, it is more fruitful to consider whether a modern democracy does not require a more expansive version of representation as its basis if it is to engage actively with the business of government, rather than merely to provide such government with a diminishing glow of legitimacy.

Here, too, there is reason to think that those early-century advocates of a pluralism that challenged the representative claims of a sovereign state had grasped an essential point. 'The idea of democracy', wrote G. D. H. Cole in 1920, 'has become almost inextricably tangled up with the idea of representative government, or rather with a particular theory of representative government based on a totally false theory of representation.'[5] What was false was the notion of an all-purpose, omnicompetent representation, of which Parliament was the worst example ('Parliament professes to represent all the citizens in all things, and therefore as a rule represents none of them in anything'); whereas genuine representation was 'always specific and functional, and never general and inclusive'.[6] This insight has been massively underdeveloped, as pluralism disappeared only to reappear much later with the same name but a very different substance.[7] A particular version of representative government has held the field (and particularly so in Britain) which has not so much neglected other versions as sat upon them.

Consider its character and consequences. Representation has been conflated to elections, which are increasingly events for professional management at ever vaster cost by a political advertising industry rather than for reflective political choice. It is the matter of a single moment, in which the winner takes the spoils and claims a general representative authority for actions taken. In Britain the spoils are especially generous, as a doctrine of Westminster sovereignty carries all before it and deals roughly with those who would impede its writ. Stripped down to its essentials, the claim to representative status turns on having won an election. This may seem reasonable enough in a rough and ready way (as elections are obviously the preferred democratic method for selecting and deselecting governments, and it is better that those who win rather than those who lose should get the prize), but it may nevertheless be judged more rough than ready.

This is not merely because the operation of the electoral system produces such blatantly unrepresentative outcomes (though it does), nor that electoral choice is massively circumscribed by the fact that the decisive choice – of candidates – has already been made by a dubiously representative party system which has redefined the nature of representation in its own image (though it has). More fundamentally, it is because representation is unduly narrowed and, thereby, distorted. It is reduced to an event, when it should be a process. It is made the matter of a moment, when it should properly be seen as continuous. It is confined to a single channel, when it should flow through a whole range of channels.

Its form is largely restricted to a single mode, when there are a wide variety of available and appropriate representative modes for different purposes.

The complexity of modern societies and the scale of their governments suggests the need for a matching system of representation if the claims of democratic governance are to be made good. In practice, of course, powerful social and economic interests do 'represent' themselves in the process of government, but this kind of covert representation compounds rather than resolves the problem of democracy. These are issues for all societies, but they present themselves in Britain in a particularly unfortunate way because of the character of its polity. There is an inherent tension between a pluralistic approach to representation and the straightjacket of sovereignty. They point towards different kinds of politics: the former towards a negotiated politics of social partnership, the latter towards a politics of *dominium*. It is not surprising, in such a political tradition, that both left and right have vigorously rejected the legitimacy of corporatist modes of representation in the name of the pure milk of parliamentary representation. But it is equally unsurprising that such a political tradition encounters particular difficulties in finding an agreed and durable basis for the achievement of social and economic objectives, and that the representative principle has atrophied into a fading badge of legitimacy when it should be the active democratic constituent of modern big government.

The fact is that governance has been given primacy over representation in Britain, but a second fact (which it is difficult not to see as a direct consequence of the first) is that such governance has not proved notably effective in enlisting social support for the twentieth-century tasks of government. This suggests the need to take representation rather more seriously than it has been taken in the past and to regard it not as an unproblematic historical achievement, but as a contemporary democratic challenge. It should be a matter of rich textures, not the thin veneer of snatched moments and single channels. It is in this sense that Raymond Williams envisaged the construction of 'complex interlocking systems' as we 'move beyond the all-purpose political unit and the all-purpose representative to a range of specific and varying political units and specific and varying representatives.'[8]

In case this sounds too unwieldy and intimidating, it is as well to be clear about what it does – and does not – mean. It does not mean a devaluation of territorial and electoral representation, but it does mean changes in its structure and operation. The opportunity exists to move to a kind of electoral system for the House of Commons which combines (though never perfectly) a number of desirable characteristics – above all, representation and governance – far more satisfactorily than is the case now. Moreover (as the Plant Report on electoral reform commissioned by the Labour Party sensibly argued),[9] different institutions serve different purposes, and it is therefore appropriate to think in terms of a variety of representative and electoral systems. The task of finally converting the House of Lords into an effective second chamber provides one obvious opportunity. However, it is also necessary to make some response to the colonization of the representative system by the political parties. If there is deemed to be a public interest, convertible into law, in the process whereby trade unions select their leaders and take their decisions, there is a more obvious public interest involved in the process whereby political parties select the candidates who become the representatives and who provide the political recruits from which political leadership is drawn. At the very least, a system of properly monitored primary elections, involving all party members on an equal basis, is required; but even this may not be enough to redress the imbalance between party and citizen representation on this front (which parallels and compounds the imbalance between representation and governance in the electoral system).

However, territorial representation (even when localized as far as possible) is anyway not enough. Citizens do not merely inhabit a territory, but live in a dense network of interests and associations. It may be convenient to contract representation into an omnibus form and a single channel, but it remains the case that representation is most effective when it is most differentiated. What this implies is a developed structure of functional representation alongside a reformed structure of territorial representation. In part, this means a structure whereby major social interests can represent themselves in government on a continuing basis, not covertly but openly and explicitly. In part, too, it means a disaggregation of representation away from over-arching structures where it is least effective and into new structures for particular functions and services (for example, policing, education or health) where it is most effective.

Nor is it necessary to regard elections as the only democratically satisfactory mode of representation. That was not the view of the classical democrats, and recent invitations to explore the merits of statistical representation for a variety of purposes should be taken seriously.[10] Statistical representation, or selection by lot, could usefully complement, even sometimes replace, the other representative devices (of election and appointment) across a range of public bodies, such as those governing schools, monitoring health services and sitting on council committees. What all this does mean, though, is a radical break with a resolutely anti-pluralist doctrine of sovereignty, which in Britain makes representation a flag of legitimacy rather than an active agency of control, and makes government stand over society rather than engage with it as an enabling partner. Doctrines matter; and it will be necessary to replace an attenuated and improbable version of representation with a richer and more plausible version if a democratic reconstruction of the British polity is really to be undertaken.

15

Reconstructions II: Accountability

> In a period when effective power in all spheres of life – economic, social, political – is being concentrated in fewer and fewer hands, parliamentary control of the executive has been steadily decreasing, without being replaced by other methods of democratic control.
>
> R. H. S. Crossman, Introduction to Walter Bagehot *The English Constitution* (1963).

Rousseau's jibe about the English only being free once every five years at least reminds us why the raw accountability of electoral democracy is not enough. It may be the bottom line; but on a day-to-day basis it is the lines above that matter more. Being able to kick parties and governments out is indispensable, but so is being able to kick them while they are in. Indeed, when put more sedately, that is precisely what the British version of representative government has conventionally been described as being about, a matter not of ruling but of checking and controlling those who rule.

It was John Stuart Mill who, in the middle of the last century, gave eloquent expression to this central function of accountability:

> Instead of the function of governing, for which it is radically unfit, the proper office of a representative assembly is to watch and control the government: to throw the light of publicity on its acts: to compel a full exposition and justification of all of them which any one considers questionable; to censure them if found condemnable, and, if the men who compose the government abuse their trust, or fulfil it in a manner which conflicts with the deliberate sense of the nation, to expel them from

office, and either expressly or virtually appoint their successors.[1]

In this way, so Mill and those who followed in his path affirmed, it was possible to maintain the integrity of the governing function as a specialized activity while also ensuring that those who governed were held to account for their actions and inactions. This could be put more directly. In a system of 'strong' government, such as that in Britain, there should also be a system of 'strong' accountability.

Now accountability is undoubtedly a 'chameleon word',[2] with an exasperating ability to slip between a whole range of meanings and carrying all the conceptual burdens of its long history. There are all the difficulties involved in separating (but also linking) managerial and political versions of accountability; narrow but indispensable traditions of financial accounting with other and larger traditions; and weaker political versions (of giving retrospective accounts of actions taken) with stronger versions (as with Mill's watching and controlling) in which there are real sanctions and penalties in play. Cutting through the conceptual maze, though, the essential fact is that in Britain strong government is not paralleled by strong accountability, but by its absence.

Equally, the reconstructive principle is clear: continuously functioning big government should be accompanied by effective and continuous mechanisms for holding government to account. The principle has only to be stated for the gap between nineteenth-century theory and twentieth-century practice to be apparent. The model of a representative assembly actively and energetically calling government to account meets the reality of a 'craven' Parliament reduced to the role of 'heckling the steamroller'.[3] The supplementary devices employed to ensure financial rectitude in the world of minimal government have not only proved ineffectual as a means of exercising similar control today, but this narrowed version of financial accountability has not itself been supplemented by the range of mechanisms appropriate to the expanded and complex world of big government and quasi-government. The fact that the poll tax could be advanced as the solution to the problem of accountability in local government provides dismal testimony to this.

It is not just that the traditional doctrines about accountability are inadequate, but that they positively get in the way of new approaches. This can be seen on a number of fronts. For as long as it is claimed that Parliament is the place where governments are held to account, or the grievances of citizens against public power redressed, so it becomes harder to develop a network of additional channels of a systematic and coherent kind. For as long as a doctrine of ministerial responsibility can be marshalled, not to hold ministers to account (except as a constitutional fiction) but to envelop the bureaucracy in a black cloud of non-accountability, so it is made more difficult to open up to scrutiny the decision-making process. For as long as the doctrine of parliamentary sovereignty affirms that the rights of citizens cannot be guaranteed against Parliament, but only *through* Parliament, so the protection of such rights in law is necessarily blocked.

Nor is this all. A further blockage arises from the extent to which the fact of election has traditionally been offered as a fact about accountability. More precisely, it has been offered as the 'democratic' solution to the problem of accountability: he who says election says accountability. On this view, issues of accountability arise only in relation to those parts of government which are not elected.[4] Yet this is patently not the case. Indeed, the irony may be that this comfortable belief actually diminishes the pursuit of accountability on the part of the elected (with the additional irony that the absence of this belief on the part of the non-elected may even be a spur to accountability). This was precisely the conclusion of one study of members of a number of elected and non-elected public bodies:

> The paradox would seem to be that the rhetoric of election as synonymous with accountability may, in fact, divert attention from the conditions that have to be met if accountability in the full sense is to be achieved; in contrast, members who lack the legitimacy of election appear to be more conscious of their need for control.[5]

It is always sensible to keep in mind Walt Whitman's line about 'the never-ending audacity of elected persons', especially of those in power.

A similar elective audacity has been apparent in the attitude of those who have set their face against any attempt to give legal status and protection to the basic rights of citizenship (whether through the modest step of the incorporation of the European Convention or the more radical alternative of a domestic bill of rights). The difficulties here are evident enough. There *is* a problem about entrenchment in relation to parliamentary sovereignty, but the problem belongs to parliamentary sovereignty. There *is* a problem about the judges in relation to rights (memorably summarized by Lord Atkin in *Liversidge v. Anderson* (1942) as judges being 'more executive-minded than the executive'), but that points attention to the need to modernize the judiciary. What should not be a problem, though, is the recognition that a democracy can properly want to entrench certain basic rights of citizenship as a defence against arbitrary government (even if that government possesses a parliamentary majority), nor that such a democracy should also want to establish and entrench constitutional securities in a new, codified constitution.[6] The argument that a democracy is distinguished by the ease with which a majority (usually, of course, a minority) can get its way – that a doctrine of electoral accountability trumps any doctrines of legal and constitutional accountability – is really an argument for a particular kind of democracy. The kind, in fact, represented by Britain's elective dictatorship.

It is possible, of course, that the need for radical constitutional surgery to institutionalize a range of accountabilities would be obviated by a return to a political culture in which governments played by the unwritten rules (with the Thatcher period regarded as an aberration), underpinned always by the back-stop of electoral accountability. Even if this was thought to be inadequate, it would still be possible to stiffen up existing arrangements if a government was prepared to introduce a range of measures designed to limit its freedom of action with respect to certain basic rights and constitutional fundamentals. This, in essence, has been the approach and the promise of the Labour Party in recent times.[7] Even more securely, it might be the case that Parliament itself would assert its accountability function with renewed vigour and give the executive a much harder time than in the modern past, especially in political conditions (note the benefits on this front resulting from the diminished Conservative majority after the 1992 General Election) where parliamentary majorities had to be won rather than merely summoned.

Unfortunately, all these possibilities have their problems. The Thatcher period did not invent executive domination nor the accelerating bias against accountability in the system (as Crossman's remarks in the early 1960s clearly indicate), but what it did do was to demonstrate that the ghost was well and truly out of the cupboard. It is unlikely that a party or a government, even one equipped with a self-denying ordinance on the matter of executive domination, will find it easy to provide assurances that the cupboard can again be securely locked. That assurance could be provided by a reinvigorated Parliament. In Peter Hennessy's words: 'If Parliament is supine, all manner of accountabilities don't work.'[8] This is why so much attention over the years has been devoted to suggesting ways in which Parliament could be 'reformed' in order that its accountability function could be strengthened in relation to an increasingly powerful executive. However, this is also why, as its partisan function consistently snuffs out any real development of its accountability function, some at least of these putative parliamentary reformers have turned from internal reform to external reform.[9] Issues about accountability necessarily mesh with issues about representation.

Yet there is no difficulty in assembling a long list of ways (many of them thoroughly stale in the telling) whereby parliamentary control of the executive could be strengthened. Ultimately it is only Parliament that can refuse to be rolled over routinely by governments in a legislative process that has become increasingly shoddy; and only Parliament that can decide to hassle rather than merely heckle the steamroller. It is extraordinary (to take an example that is less notorious than it should be) that a democratic Parliament has not taken steps to claim for itself a range of prerogative powers – including the power of war and peace – that governments have acquired from the Crown but not bequeathed to an elected assembly, or that it has not taken steps to exercise some control over the vast volume of patronage appointments at the disposal of ministers, or that it has not insisted on its rights of access and scrutiny in relation to those activities of government (most notably, the security services and the whole apparatus of what has been aptly described as the 'secret state') where it has been firmly excluded. A vigorous Parliament could move on all these fronts, just as it could decide to beef up the scrutiny powers and resources of its select committees, bring civil servants decisively within the arena of accountability, and (the perennial point) undertake the kind of overhaul of its procedure, facilities and organization that would turn it from a declining club to a modern assembly.

With or without the framework of accountability provided by

a written constitution and a bill of rights, it is upon Parliament that the continuous and detailed responsibility for holding government to account necessarily falls. If Parliament fails in that responsibility (as it largely does now), then no amount of constitutional underpinning can fill the gap. Yet it is a remarkable fact that those who have waxed most lyrical about the role of Parliament (and of the parliamentarian) have also been those who have most resisted attempts to enhance its actual ability to scrutinize and control the activities of big government.[10] They may, though, have a point, even if not quite the one they intended. It is simply not plausible (even leaving aside its essentially partisan character) to expect Parliament to be the unique constitutional instrument of accountability in relation to modern government. The belief that this was (and had to be) so has made it difficult to develop effective additional instruments. There are, of course, a number of crucial informal instruments whereby accountability is pressed (notably through the activities of the opposition party and of the media, with varying effectiveness),[11] but Parliament dominates the high ground of formal constitutional accountability while finding it ever more difficult to fill the obvious chasm between constitutional theory and political and administrative practice.

The way out of this impasse is not for Parliament to seek to reclaim a function it cannot discharge, certainly not alone, but to put in place the measures and machinery designed to ensure that the range and complexity of big government is matched by an equal range and complexity in the techniques of accountability. In other words, not to seek to do what it cannot do, but to make sure that what has to be done is done.[12] The example of the Ombudsman points in one direction; that of the National Audit Office in another. Inspectorates may not be exciting, but they too should be seen as integral to the operation of accountable government. As the regulatory state expands, as the institutions of quasi-government proliferate, and as the interpenetration of public and private power proceeds apace, blurring both traditional accounts of how government works and of how it is held to democratic account, it becomes urgent and important to ensure that the governmental process at every level is firmly embedded in a system of continuously functioning accountability. A recent proposal that the 'rule of law' should be understood in terms of a 'reconstitutionalization of the business of governing' (and translated into a British Administrative Procedure Act) is an inelegant but interesting example of how this could be undertaken on a wide front,[13] but a whole range of more specific initiatives are also available.

The difficulty is not in finding the way, but in summoning the will. It is ironic that at the end of the 1980s the Conservative Government chose to fly the flag of accountability in relation to public services at the very period when there was widespread unease about the lack of accountability in British government itself. However, the way in which it raised the flag, revealing a partisan, unbalanced and non-negotiated view of what a process of accountability properly involves, also reflected precisely the problem at the heart of the British system of government. Accountability is too important to be defined by governments or majority parties. Through a plethora of channels and a multitude of devices, it should be in the bloodstream of the polity. The task for Parliament, and for people, is to put it there – and to keep it pumping away.

16

Reconstructions III: Participation

Any participation, even in the smallest public function, is
useful . . .
John Stuart Mill *Considerations on Representative Government*
(1861)

That view of democracy (sometimes described as the 'classical'
view) which emphasizes the importance of the opportunities
afforded to citizens for active participation in public affairs has
not found much favour in Britain, either in theory or practice. Of
course, the view itself has had a bad century, as larger democratic
ambitions have been reined in on the basis of anxious readings of
the modern condition,[1] but this kind of contraction was already
firmly entrenched in British political culture. The British tradition
was a governing tradition, and its citizens (properly, subjects)
were not required or expected, wars always excepted, to exert
themselves in strenuous civic activity. It was important to die for
the state; but living for it was another matter.

No doubt this is put much too baldly and abbreviates a complex
history. It does, nevertheless, touch an aspect of the British political tradition and one that conditions much else. Here is both a
barrier to democratic advance and a condition of such advance. It
is a reminder that even the best and most democratic of constitutions will only be as good as the soil in which they are planted;
and that, in this respect at least, British soil is historically under-
nourished. It has been deliberately under-nourished by a Tory
tradition which emphasized governing as a specialized activity to
be done by those (pre-eminently themselves) who knew how to
do it, and which was preoccupied with ensuring that new entrants
to the system from without could be trusted to govern on the

old terms. This seemed unlikely in the twentieth century, as the labour movement appeared destined to translate its ideology of democratic self-government, reflected in a dense network of participatory institutions, into a new kind of state and new structural forms. As it turned out, though, not merely did this not happen, but in so far as the central and local state substituted itself for voluntaristic self-help across tracts of social and economic life, without at the same time developing new forms of participation and control, the top was strengthened while the bottom was weakened. The social and economic basis of citizenship had been enhanced; but there was no similar nourishment for the practice of citizenship.

This has produced occasional laments, but only at two moments in this century has something more substantial been presaged. The first moment, in the second decade of the century, has already been noticed, when from several directions there was a concerted, though ultimately abortive, attempt to widen and deepen the expression of democracy beyond that acknowledged by a doctrine of sovereignty. The second moment bridged the 1960s and 1970s, when a widespread demand for increased citizen participation entered the official culture for a time (with the landmark Skeffington Report on the planning system in 1969 defining participation as 'the act of sharing in the formulation of policies and proposals')[2] and generated both a huge literature and a raft of initiatives across the length and breadth of public administration. However, the moment passed and, as a colder economic climate set in, the verdict on the period seemed to be that: 'Little has been achieved by way of a fundamental shift in power, a shift which implicitly underlay the ideas of radical proponents of participation in the late 1960s.'[3]

Some of these ideas deserved to wither, in so far as they carried with them dangerously unrealistic assumptions about the ability to dispense with representative institutions and substitute in their place a direct democracy of endlessly participating citizenry. However, there is also much to be retrieved and built on, not least the understanding that it is both possible and desirable to supplement the institutions of representative democracy with arenas and opportunities for the active exercise of citizenship – and that this is the more necessary in a polity where such opportunities have been in traditionally short supply. It is quite possible to combine a lack of illusions about the difficulties of participation (for example, the 'inverse law of participation – that those with the greatest need to push their own interests have the least capacity to do so effectively')[4] with a recognition that it is not in such difficulties that the British failure to travel far down the participatory road is to be found. There has been much blocking the way (party ideologies, political culture, doctrines of representation and sovereignty, the professional culture of public services and much else) and little opening it up. The general character of the political system has found its reflection in the character of the administrative system.

It is not necessary, on grounds of democratic theory, to believe that participation is a 'good thing' or that, like Mill, it is a school of moral improvement both for individuals and societies, to be concerned at the meagre nature of the opportunities available to citizens to exercise some influence and control over their political, social and economic life or to be concerned about the consequences of such meagreness. There are, moreover, good reasons to think that matters are getting worse, even beyond the dominating twentieth-century fact that the state (along with the private state) has grown while the instruments of citizenship have remained the same. The nature of the electoral system increasingly acts as a disincentive to participation because of the diminished opportunity it offers to affect outcomes. Local elections have ever less connection with local decision-making as power (with money) has shifted to the centre and offer, at best, an opportunity for those who can be bothered to register a vote for or against the government of the day. More and more of the activities of government, now accounting for a fifth of all public spending, are now in the hands of appointed boards and non-democratic public bodies. The National Health Service has been severed from even the flimsiest kind of local democratic control. Those changes in the government of education that have enfranchised parents and created a quarter million army of school governors might seem to point in a different direction (and potentially do), except that they have formed part of a strategy of central control which needed local agents in the drive against local education authorities and professional interests. It is scarcely surprising therefore that so many school governors seem not to know what their role is, or should be.[5] Meanwhile, on another front, even tentative developments towards worker participation in industry have been officially aborted (although Europe may secure resuscitation), while in those

public institutions where participatory decision-making was traditionally strong (as in universities) it has largely been replaced
by more robust management styles.

There is something more to add to this story. It is the political
parties that have provided the main channel for mass political
participation (beyond the act of voting), but this channel, never
very large anyway, has become much narrower as party membership has steadily declined.[6] The mass party, the invention of democratic politics, has declined as the professionalization of politics
has increased. Who but politicians need to attend to political
arguments? Who but party media-machines need to persuade and
campaign? Nor is it simply the case, as has often been suggested,
that the participatory slack has been taken up by a shift of popular
engagement towards single-issue groups of assorted kinds.
Important and vital though these are, it would not be satisfactory
to regard them as a substitute for (rather than an extension of)
that more general participation in public affairs – involving the
weighing of interests and opinions and not just the narrow pursuit
of particular ones – which is a constituent of citizenship. Moreover, the group universe has itself also become a world of professional bureaucracies (more solicitous of direct debits than of
direct democracy); while it anyway requires a kind of political
structure more open and amenable than that in Britain to a continuing engagement with the universe of opinions and interests.

So what might taking participation seriously involve? There is
no shortage of possibilities on almost every front. In terms of the
absence of structured opportunities for participation in the policy
process on the part of interested groups, it would be possible
through administrative law to provide procedural guarantees to
this effect. It has been well argued that this kind of requirement
about the nature and conduct of the policy process offers a means
of reconstituting the 'rule of law' in the context of the expanded
state.[7] Across the whole spread of central, sub-central and quasi-
government, procedural participation would sit not as (at best) a
bolt-on extra, but as a fundamental constituent of the policy
process itself. However, beyond this basic administrative underpinning there is likely to be a huge diversity in the forms and
methods of participation.

It is important to build participation into the high politics of
central state decision-making, but it is no less important that it
should form part of the texture of social life and organization

itself. Here, too, democracy is a matter of multiple levels, channels and arenas, not easily or properly compressed into a tidy monopoly. 'The real democracy that does exist in Great Britain', wrote G. D. H. Cole, 'is to be found for the most part not in Parliament or in the institutions of local government, but in the smaller groups, formal or informal, in which men and women join together out of decent fellowship or for the pursuit of a common social purpose – societies, clubs, churches, and not least, informal neighbourhood groups.'[8] This is well said, but it also invites us to consider how a range of 'common social purposes' (beyond those which merely require to be celebrated and left alone) could acquire more 'real democracy' in terms of citizen involvement than is currently provided by the institutions of central or local government.

Some of these common purposes will derive from particular roles (for example, as parents, patients, tenants, travellers, sports players) and find their focus in particular services (on the same examples, education, health, housing, transport, recreation). Others will be rooted in territory, the fact of living in a particular place. The former suggests the need to develop a variety of means at a variety of levels whereby the users of services can contribute to policy making in relation to them (while not making unrealistic assumptions about either the ease or equity of such participation). To give an example of one means at one level, the traditional assumption in the case of local government services that electoral participation through the ballot box is the mechanism of user control (perhaps supplemented by co-option on to council committees, though usually of producer rather than user interests) is clearly inadequate. It is oddly revealing that a statutory mechanism for user participation was built into the reorganized health service in the 1970s (in the shape of Community Health Councils) on the grounds that 'normal' electoral participation, as with local government services, was absent. Yet there are good grounds for thinking that user councils with statutory powers (and with interesting possibilities in terms of their composition) might have a useful role to play in relation to the whole range of local public services.[9]

In terms of place, too, the fact of neighbourhood should be built into all considerations of local government areas and modes of service delivery. Participation and control is most effective when it is within easy reach and concerns matters of which people have direct experience. Services should always be organized at the most local level possible and there should be real opportunities for effective participation (with the 'costs' of such participation, especially for weaker groups, not pitched too high). Too often these matters are approached from the wrong end or – with successive local government reviews – hardly approached at all. It is worth recalling that when the Webbs, those allegedly arch centralizers, turned their attention to the structure of government, they came to the conclusion that it was necessary to build from the bottom (in the shape of wards of 2,000 to 4,000 people) not from the top, with successive levels added for particular purposes.[10] It is not the case for decentralization that should have to be made, but the case for centralization; while it cannot be said too often that the administrative technique of decentralizing services is not the same as the political requirement for democratizing services.[11]

There is much scope for experiment and diversity, on every side and at every level, if only because existing participatory opportunities are so meagre. Reform of the electoral system should have as a central criterion the extent to which a reformed system would provide a stimulus to participation in terms of an enhanced ability to influence outcomes. However, the policy content of electoral choice would still be uncertain and imprecise, suggesting the desirability of supplementing it with other opportunities for citizens, both locally and nationally, to express policy preferences (with the referendum as one such, not as something incompatible with parliamentary sovereignty but – as Dicey himself argued – required precisely *because* of the potential for party tyranny contained within that constitutional doctrine).[12] Public funding of political parties could be linked to their ability not merely to win votes but to recruit members and engage them in democratic tasks. It is not necessary to believe in the wilder fantasies about the participatory possibilities of new technology to think that some progress could also be made on this front.[13]

More generally, government (both national and local) needs to become the active sponsor of new ways of running a range of public services and institutions. In some respects (as with the *Next Steps* programme in the civil service) this is precisely what is happening, but in ways which deliberately dodge questions about participation and accountability. As Bernard Crick wrote in the 1970s:

The most likely prophecy of common trends in the future, is that things will get both bigger and smaller. It will not be the vanishing of central government that is likely, but the devolution to localities, unions, industries or professions and schools of more and more decisions – decisions subject to final central control, but whose initiative and form are local.[14]

We now know, better than we knew then, that there are very different terms upon which such a process can be undertaken. Some can enhance and strengthen citizenship (by promoting participation, developing user control, finding new ways to combine producer, consumer and public interests, buttressing lay endeavour with professional support), others can undermine it. However, we also know something more than we did then about the perils and consequences of cutting people adrift from the bonds of citizenship.

17

Reconstructions IV: Openness

> Another aspect of this tradition is the general agreement that
> it is better not to probe too deeply when things go wrong.
> A. H. Birch *Representative and Responsible Government* (1964)

It might seem unnecessary to have to argue that a modern democracy should have a commitment to openness as one of its basic
ingredients. Certainly it should be unnecessary. It may not be
quite the case, as Francis Bacon famously put it, that 'knowledge
itself is power', but that they are intimately connected is something of which there can be no real doubt. That is clearly the
view of governments and the powerful, since they have always
regarded the control of information as a major preoccupation. In
this matter too, though, the general case has a distinctively British
application and, because of that, acquires a particular significance.

The central fact, now thoroughly stale in the telling, is that the
British way of governing has been characterized by an extraordinary secrecy, unrivalled amongst comparable Western democracies. One testimony, the more remarkable because it comes
from a former Whitehall permanent secretary, may stand for
many: the 'culture of secrecy is bred in the bone of British parliamentary democracy'.[1] Lord Hailsham once provided a convenient
public school translation: 'Thou shalt not blub, and thou shalt not
sneak'.[2] What this has meant for British democracy (and for British society) has been exhaustively recorded. It ranges far and wide,
high and low. For most of the twentieth century the Official
Secrets Act (nodded through in a day in 1911) has enveloped the
whole of public life in a blanket of official secrecy; and when its
notorious catch-all section two was finally reformed, after a mere
eighty years, by the 1989 Official Secrets Act, not only did this

new legislation continue to allow ample scope for continued prose-
cutions (above all, by its specific exclusion of a public interest
defence) but was emphatically not intended to form part of a
widening of access to official information.

However, this is anyway merely the visible tip of a much larger
iceberg. As the succession of *causes célèbres* of the 1980s showed,
British governments have equipped themselves with a formidable
repertoire of devices to employ against whistle-blowing civil servants, journalists and broadcasters. At their heart is the ability of
ministers of the Crown to sustain the claim that there is an
identity between the interests of the state and the policies of the
government of the day; and the absence in public law of a recognized interest of state by reference to which disclosure can be
compelled and information revealed. The position was admirably,
and appallingly, summarized by McCowan J. in the trial of civil
servant Clive Ponting:

> We have General Elections in this country. The majority party
> in the House of Commons forms the Government. If it loses
> majority support it ceases to do so, but for the time being, it
> *is* the Government, and its policies are those of the State.[3]

But this 'high' secrecy only forms one part of that routine web
of secrecy that envelops the workings of government in Britain.
Behind the particular practices there is a whole culture. Thus the
cabinet committee structure has been kept from view while leaks
and lobby lubricate the system.[4] Official statistics can be doctored[5]
and, as the annual opening of the thirty-year rule cabinet archive
regularly reveals, ministers devote much of their effort to keeping
information out of the public domain. Even routine information
collected by government about standards of products and services
is withheld, while some information of this kind can only be
obtained from foreign governments.[6]

Yet, as James Cornford puts it, the present situation is 'certainly
consonant with our constitutional tradition'.[7] That is precisely the
point. An executive-dominated constitution, in which ministers
have inherited prerogative powers from the Crown, is not one
which has been accustomed to sharing information with citizens
or their representatives. To have done so would have been to
govern in a different kind of way; indeed, to have been a different
kind of government. Instead, constitutional doctrines are advanced
to explain why matters are conducted as they are and why, in

constitutional terms, no significant change is permissible or desirable. The central doctrine is that of ministerial responsibility, whereby ministers alone are answerable to Parliament for what departments do and civil servants are preserved in their virginal state of anonymous neutrality. This chain of accountability would be broken if there were more windows on the policy process and a linchpin of responsible constitutional government thereby kicked away. The problem with this argument is that it amounts to saying it is necessary to keep certain fictions intact if a traditional theory of the constitution is to be maintained.

The root fiction (and deceit) lies in the way in which a doctrine of ministerial responsibility is marshalled to defend a politics of secrecy despite the fact that effective responsibility – the promise of the doctrine – is thereby undercut.[8] In other words, the doctrine is invoked in the service of its exact opposite. For the truth is that ministers, the monopolists of information, can decide what to disclose and what to conceal, so that the extent of secrecy is the greatest secret of all. A further truth is that the ability of Parliament to compel the executive to lay papers before the House was actually much greater in the last century, when the role of government was restricted, than in the party-dominated big government of this century. A doctrine of responsibility which denies access to the sources of information required to make responsibility effective stands matters on their head. It also sustains a whole series of further fictions: that ministers can actually be responsible for what departments do (they clearly cannot, in the sense of knowing everything that is going on) and that civil servants are not an integral part of the policy-making process (they clearly are, as their diminished anonymity and increased politicization recognizes).

Thus an evidently implausible and threadbare constitutional doctrine is deployed to maintain a veil of secrecy over the policy process and the operation of government. The costs, in democratic terms, are considerable (and in effectiveness terms too, in so far as policy advice and options are not opened up to critical scrutiny). There is abundant evidence of major policy decisions, the stuff of democratic choice, being taken by governments without Parliament or people knowing the facts of the case.[9] Equally, it is difficult to enlist people for a politics of participation in relation to a whole range of issues if there is not a parity of access to the information necessary for effective participation. Government is embedded in a dense network of interests, groups and lobbies, but the operation of this world is largely hidden from democratic view. Government also holds vast amounts of records about its citizens, but most of this cannot be accessed by the citizens themselves. All this, and more, is what the choice between open and closed government is about.

There is, though, a further choice to be made, even by those who are persuaded of the need for greater openness. This is the choice between nudging governments to let a little more light in here and there or seeking to effect a more structural change in the architecture of the constitution. The nudging approach has gains to its credit (as with the access provisions in the ombudsman and audit systems) and more can doubtless be achieved (for example, in the powers available to select committees, or in revisions to the civil service internal code). Certainly the pressures towards greater openness are likely to increase and, if only to stave off more fundamental changes (the motive which informed the Croham Directive in the civil service in the late 1970s aimed at making more documents publicly available), governments will have to continue to respond. The Major Government's 'open government initiative' is one such response. The problem with this approach, though, is that governments will continue to respond on their own terms. The executive will still decide how much information – and of what kind – it will give to its citizens or their Parliament. It was noticeable, in this context, that the information explosion promised in the Citizen's Charter in relation to certain public services was conspicuously not to apply to the activities of government itself.[10]

This is why it is necessary to reverse the relationship between government and people in the matter of information. If the present relationship accurately reflects a constitution in which the executive is dominant, so an altered relationship should be seen as an essential element in a democratic remodelling of the constitution. The presumption should be in favour of openness. Governments should have to make a case for not disclosing certain kinds of information rather than, as now, disclosing only what they choose. The shift in onus here is crucial. It is what lies at the heart of proposals for freedom of information legislation. Such legislation, common in other democracies, has been consistently resisted in Britain by governments of both major parties (as with the Government's sabotage of the Right to Know Bill in 1993).[11] The detail of any legislation is clearly important. It is necessary, through a set of exemptions, to balance openness against the proper requirement for secrecy in certain areas of government activity. However, experience elsewhere in a variety of constitutional systems indicates, not merely that this can be accomplished, but that it is accomplished in a remarkably similar way:

> The common features of all such freedom of information legislation are first, the creation of public rights of access to official information, second, that those rights are determinable and enforceable by an authority independent of government, third, that those rights extend to all official information other than that specified to be exempt, and fourth, that the exempt categories largely coincide.[12]

Thus the real resistance to such legislation in Britain is not narrowly technical (though sometimes presented as though it was), but constitutional and cultural. The absence of freedom of information provisions is rooted in a larger democratic deficit. The acquisition of such provisions would likewise both signal and herald a wider shift in the polity. Although their most visible impact, as elsewhere, would be seen in the ability of citizens to access their files and to pursue claims against government agencies, the wider impact would touch every corner of the political system. It would be necessary to think freshly about the whole process whereby public records are kept and archives maintained. Nor would it be possible for other matters – the independence and integrity of official statistics, the publication of research sponsored by government departments, the laws of confidence and contempt – which are currently a cause for concern to remain immune from the drive towards greater openness.

The consequences of such developments are clear, which explains why governments (and putative governments) have traditionally been so determined to maintain the status quo in the matter of information, calling in aid the available constitutional orthodoxies. For what is at stake is a major dent in executive power and a fundamental alteration in the balance of constitutional relationships. The reason why governments have been so hostile to greater openness (and have wanted, when pressed, to urge a policy of incremental adjustments rather than legislative enact-

ments) is precisely the reason why democratic citizens should
support it. In making life more uncomfortable for governments,
it throws a welcome searchlight on the policy process. The scrutiny role of Parliament, and of the select committees, is greatly
strengthened. The fourth estate – of both print and broadcast
journalists – is better equipped to perform the democratic role of
investigative vigilance traditionally ascribed to it, but for which
it has been substantially disabled. Citizens are better able to see,
and evaluate, what is being done in their name.

Even more than this, though, there is a beneficial impact on the
policy process itself. Government 'in the sunshine' (as openness
provisions in the United States are aptly described) becomes a
different kind of government. It becomes possible for more effective participation on the part of groups across a whole range of
issues on the basis of access to the information upon which public
policy decisions are being made. Equally, though, it enables citizens to see the groups with which government is consorting and
the terms on which such consorting is being done. If some form
of corporatist arrangement is an appropriate reflection of an
enlarged view of representation, it matters crucially that it should
be in the form of an open corporatism in which the participants
are clearly identified and their relations with government open to
public scrutiny. At the moment, by contrast, the real nature of
government is obscured from view by an ideology that denies the
interconnectedness of public and private power that is its real
nature, by a secrecy underpinning the operation of government,
and by a constitutional doctrine that explains why things are –
and must be – as they are.

What is at issue here, at bottom, is the extent to which there
is a public interest, a citizen interest, distinct from the interest of
governments or parties and needing to be built into the process of
politics and government. Much of the dissatisfaction with British
constitutional arrangements turns on their failure sufficiently to
acknowledge and incorporate this distinction. The matter of secrecy (and openness) is central to this. A closed policy process –
with the consequences that 'there is no official voice outside Parliament that provides a continuing critique of how well government
is working'[13] – is not only likely to lead to bad policies, because
untested in their preparation by adequate scrutiny and debate, but
is a standing denial that there is a legitimate citizen interest in the
process of government. Democracy is about process and product;

decision rules but also process rules. The lack of openness, a basic process rule, reflects the larger and longer character of the British governing tradition. Its effect is writ large in the conduct of politics itself. An adversarial politics of easy answers takes the place of a more difficult politics of questioning and learning. A more open kind of government is certainly a threat to that.

18

The end of politics?

Democracy is today more acutely threatened in Britain than in
any other country of parliamentary democracy.

Eric Hobsbawm *Politics for a Rational Left* (1989)

Any attempt to 'reconstruct' British politics has to be set against
the background of what is actually happening. We have to start
from where we are; and where we are is not very promising. If
it was just the case that recent history (less euphemistically, the
Thatcher Governments of the 1980s) had taught the lesson that
there were too few constraints on executive power in Britain and
that constitutional adjustments of various kinds were therefore
required to restore the balance of the constitution, the task would
be formidable enough. In fact, matters are altogether more
serious.

In part, this is for some of the reasons already discussed. It can
not simply be a matter of adjustment or restoration when both
constitutional and political traditions, and a political culture, have
provided the soil in which recent executive growth has taken
place. It may have had exceptional vigour, but it did not come
from aberrant root stock. It exploited a political tradition; it did
not subvert it. It is necessary to keep this in mind as a precaution
against thinking that a touch on the constitutional tiller will be
enough to put the polity back on course. The argument here is
that, in democratic terms, it has been off course for a very long
time. What has to be reconstructed is not some mythical pre–1979
golden age of democratic politics, but an altogether more secure
basis upon which such a politics can be built.

Yet this is only part of the reason why, in present circumstances, it is a far from straightforward enterprise. Any account

would be incomplete if it did not pay attention to another part of the picture, potentially more fundamental and far reaching in its implications. For there is already a process of reconstruction underway and quite far advanced, leading in a direction and towards a destination very different from that espoused here. It is a process in which the nature of politics itself is being redefined and reconstructed. Taking advantage of the exceptional opportunities offered to a British government with a secure majority by the constitution, it has been possible over a long period of uninterrupted rule for a party not merely to press its own policies but also its own view of politics (or anti-politics).

There is room for disagreement about the extent to which 'the world since 1979'[1] was the product of a coherent ideological mission or was made up as it went along, about the assorted sources of New Right doctrine and how this was translated into a political strategy.[2] What there is less room for disagreement about is the effect and implication of what was done. The unifying animus (whether from free marketeers or from the theorists of public choice) was against a 'political' way of taking decisions, making allocations and running services, on the grounds (and here again different arguments could be adduced from different sources) that this involved an illiberal imposition of a particular view of what was good for people, that it was inefficient, and that it was taken over by sectional interests and self-regarding bureaucracies. The task, therefore, was to expand those areas of life in which decisions were taken by markets (or quasi-markets) and contract those areas of life in which politics held sway.

Here, then, was the answer to the 'problem' of democracy, as this had long been described in New Right doctrine. It was a matter of contracting the sphere in which democratic politics would operate and making a progressive substitution of individual, consumer and market decision-making. However, the protagonists of this view themselves had doubts about whether it could be done, whatever its desirability, for this was itself part of the democratic problem. It involved a revolution of diminishing expectations as far as politics was concerned and it was far from certain that this could be accomplished. The extent to which it was accomplished is a measure of the Thatcherite achievement in terms of statecraft. However, its implications go wider and deeper.

For what the process involves, as Zygmunt Bauman has put it, is an invitation to 'exit from politics' as a response to a rapidly changing social order:

> To the new difficulty with translating human concerns into political programmes, it responds by promoting the exit of human concerns from politics. It responds to the resistance of local and group interests by casting such interests off the limits of the political agenda. It offers the public a massive programme of *buying oneself out*, singly or severally, from politics; or making politics irrelevant to the pursuit of individual or collective goals and ideas. This dismantling of effective citizenship is presented as the triumph of freedom; as liberation. What makes such presentation credible is the parallel reduction of political power to the role of a purely constraining force, and an emphatic surrender of its *enabling* function. . . . Politics is not where you invest your hopes. Life is elsewhere. Politics is a nuisance. The less of it the better.[3]

Citizens can get down to the serious business of turning themselves into consumers. The future – their future, and the collective future – is to be found in the pavilioned splendour of the shopping mall, not in the derelict remains of a traditional politics. Of course, this prospect comes to look more convincing and alluring precisely to the extent that markets do replace politics in practice over larger tracts of social life.

This is a corrective to the view that Conservative politics since 1979 has not been much bothered with constitutional issues, perhaps oddly when set against an expressed desire to rein back the state. The fact is that something far more ambitious has been undertaken; not with the constitution as the target (for that provided the indispensable means), but politics and citizenship itself. Far from wanting to convert subjects into citizens by constitutional means, a further erosion of citizenship was to be accomplished by converting politics into the realm of the subject-consumer. Already without citizen status in relation to the constitution, the subject was now to be weaned off those collective public institutions whose existence and vigour had once been cited as effective substitutes for the absence of a constitutional *guarantisme*.

Of course, the process is incomplete and may remain so (or be put into reverse). But the audacity of the enterprise has dominated recent British politics and it is as well to be clear about what it involves. It certainly represents a solution to the 'problem' of democracy (and of politics) by removing public institutions from collective political decision and forms of political accountability and substituting in their place assorted forms of market account- ability. The corollary of the removal of public activities and services from collective political accountability is the removal of the need for those arenas and mechanisms through which political decision-making takes place. In terms of its own brutal logic, therefore, once local government (to take the leading example) is stripped of its traditional service functions as these are put out to the market, it is but a short step to suggest that only an attenuated and depoliticized structure need remain.[4]

In this New Right prospectus, glimpsed and framed during a period in the 1980s when political dominance opened up large ideological vistas, the vision was of a post-collectivist despatch of politics equivalent to that post-capitalist eradication of politics once envisaged by the Marxist left.[5] For the latter it could be replaced by administration; for the former by markets. However, while one of these dangerous positions is happily dead, the other is unhappily well. It invites us to dispense with representative democracy as the means whereby a range of public activities are conducted, offers a 'participation without politics'[6] as economic man is substituted for political man, and dissolves traditional forms of political accountability. 'Britain is the only country in the western world', wrote one distinguished commentator in the late 1980s, 'whose government could allow itself to think in these terms.'[7]

Not merely to think in such terms, but to translate thought into action on a number of fronts. The tension between democracy and efficiency is a permanent tension in democratic government, but what was new was the way in which the tension was resolved (across a range of policy areas) by deliberately taking democracy out of the account.[8] This was as true of the administrative reforms as it was of the approach to urban or social policy. Democratic politics as a negotiated and accountable public activity to which tests of public interest could be applied was to be replaced wher- ever possible by four alternative models. The first was of a mana- gerialism armed with the hard stuff of performance indicators and freed from the restraints of political interference. The second was of public institutions and services increasingly taking their charac- ter from the extent to which their activities are traded and marketed. The third was of post-collectivist man using his individual resources to make choices from the range of available suppliers, defining, extracting and (increasingly) purchasing his own needs without collective determination. The fourth was of traditional political structures being replaced by new 'intermediate institutions' of various kinds in relation to particular activities.

The common thread running through these various approaches was a dissolution of political accountability. The sledgehammer of sovereignty was deployed by the centre to tighten its own grip on a range of public activities, loosen the grip of others who might claim a rival legitimacy, and change the terms on which the activities were to be conducted. The less that such activities were conducted by bodies based upon a general representative basis, then the less it was either appropriate or possible for forms of accountability associated with such bodies to survive. It would increasingly be managers rather than politicians who would take distributional and allocational decisions, and this meant that managerial and financial, rather than political, forms of accountability would properly apply. Indeed, accountability becomes increasingly invisible as the terms on which public activities are conducted are made to correspond to market conditions. As the familiar characteristics of the economic market (that 'nobody decides' and nobody is to blame) are extended to areas of former political decision-making, then similar claims can be made in these areas too. Under this new dispensation the task of the 'intermediate' institutions charged with responsibility in these areas is not to define a public interest but to respond to market signals.

Indeed, the very notion of a public interest, underpinning the distinctiveness of the arrangements and purposes whereby 'public' services are conducted, is called into question. The public interest ceases to be a matter of democratic decision and political accountability and becomes the outcome of a whole series of private decisions and private interests for which no particular responsibility can be attributed. Ministers are able to shrug off responsibility by pointing to the fact that decisions are being taken by devolved budget-holders of various kinds who are more or less efficient in their market behaviour; other erstwhile representative bodies (such as health authorities, education authorities and local government in general) can properly plead diminished responsibility on the grounds of attenuated function and enforced incapacity; while the devolved agencies themselves rightly point out that they are only operating according to the rules imposed on them – rules they did not invent.

Education provides a good example of the general case. Its post-war progress has been charted in terms of a passage from a 'professional' to a 'market' version of accountability.[9] In seeking to break the professional model, the market version has combined rigid central control (at the expense not just of professional autonomy but of local democracy) with a funding formula for schools based not on need but on market position and to be applied by empowered school governors. It is a system in which a certain amount of ideological re-education is required (until parents, schools and governors come to believe that they no longer have any responsibilities for other schools and other children) and in which accountability is elusive and (as school governors as the new intermediaries are discovering) is not the same as power. The governor who joins to 'support the school' but is asked to decide which teacher to sack may stand as the paradigm case of accountability without power in a market model.

But the end of politics? On one side, the prospect is of the market, where people are 'free' but unaccountable power rules, extending its reach to areas of 'public' activity traditionally ordered through political forms of decision and accountability. There will be less for politics to do and more for the market to do. On the other side, the process is presided over by a state which, as in Britain, has developed its own political version of power without accountability. The combined effect has been described as a system of 'dual rule', of market and state, with 'the role of democracy in such a state . . . that of a plebiscite which legitimizes the actions of the administration'.[10] It is a system in which politics count for less and less, but in which the winner takes more and more.

19

Becoming citizens

> What is this citizenship that everyone keeps talking about?
> Melanie Phillips 'Citizenship sham in our secret society',
> *Guardian*, 14 September 1990

Actions give rise to reactions. The exit from politics has met resistance and obstruction from those unwilling to abandon democratic territory to the combined forces of state and market and their pincer movement of non-accountable decision making. The resistance has found common ground in the idea of citizenship, which established a ubiquitous presence in the language of British politics at the end of the 1980s. This was a remarkable and revealing development, reflecting a widespread sense that it was a period of exceptional political significance when the entire character of the polity was at issue. It was appropriate, therefore, that a contemporary resonance should be sought for an ancient word which defined the nature of a political community.

However, the definition had always been contested, and so it remained.[1] For the Thatcherites citizenship was a no-nonsense doctrine about personal and social responsibility, the basis for sermons and exhortations about the duties of individuals and families. As such it could be called in aid (as it was constantly at the Conservative Conference in 1988) to buttress the shift from politics to markets. A gloss was added by those Conservatives who felt uncomfortable – and, perhaps, vulnerable – in the company of a rampant individualism that cut people adrift from wider social engagements. Thus was born the 'active citizen', allegedly deactivated in the past by the suffocating grip of collectivist bureaucracy, but now energized by the new climate of voluntarism and finding rich pastures for worthy social endeavour as parent governors, neighbourhood watchers and victim supporters (though, revealingly, political parties, let alone trade unions or issue groups, were never included in such lists of participatory worthiness).[2]

Whether in its raw or glossed version, here was a new citizenship for the new times. Offered as an account of citizenship, it was really a substitute for it. As Neal Ascherson observed:

> It at once emerges that the activity of the active citizens is to pick up the victims of the free market and the swimming survivors of the sunken Welfare State. The blow must fall first. There's no place here for independent social groups which try to deflect the blow before it connects.[3]

What was on offer was a privatization of citizenship, removed from its ancestral place in the public realm – where it defined common purposes and structured public activities – and ushered into a private realm of charitable works and voluntary endeavour (all of course admirable in themselves) where it would not interfere with the business of 'real' politics.

Yet citizenship is irredeemably public. It is about what it means to be a citizen and a community of citizens. Its emphasis upon the civic is a standing reminder that social life is more than a maelstrom of atomic individualism and that individuals themselves have a social character that is not reducible to a bundle of private interests. In emphasizing the social grounding of rights and obligations, it involves a denial that these can be matters of purely private determination. Furthermore, citizenship is active in the sense that it makes public affairs everyone's concern, the activity of ruling and being ruled at the same time, not to be confused with the passivity of subjecthood (for 'whilst all citizens are subjects, not all subjects are citizens').[4] In the relationship that is governing, the citizen is a participant while the subject is a recipient. The difference matters.

Thus the skirmishing around the idea of citizenship in recent British politics turns on more than a word, to be appropriated variously according to taste. On one side, it was an idea to be remodelled in line with the new market individualism, stripped of its collective dimension and repainted as the extramural pursuit of consumers and producers. On another side, though, it has provided the ground upon which the line against the prevailing ideological tendencies could be held and counter-attacks essayed.

This has a number of aspects, with some tensions and disagreements, but all pointing towards a contemporary definition of citizenship in a modern democratic context radically different from its privatized version.

There is, crucially, the recognition that the subjects of the British state need to acquire the attributes of citizenship and that this involves a process of radical constitutional reform. The notion that custom and practice on the part of the practitioners of politics adequately fills the gaps left by the absence of constitutional provisions regarding the rights of individuals or the relations between institutions can no longer be sustained, nor can the belief that there need be no distinction made between ordinary legislation and the law of the constitution. The much-vaunted 'flexibility' of the system is also the sledgehammer of sovereignty, an executive property wearing the legitimating clothes of parliamentarianism. All this was clearer at the end of the 1980s than it had been at the beginning, but it was, nevertheless, not the errant product of that bleak decade but a basic feature of a system (and of its supporting ideologies) in which governing was prized more than accountability. Whatever their particular disagreements, constitutional reformers were agreed on the need to correct that pivotal imbalance.

The task, though, was not just to insert some old-fashioned constitutionalism into the system, necessary though that was, but to think freshly about how the growth and operation of big government could be matched by the techniques of democracy. This suggested the need to think of democracy in complex, plural and variegated terms, with a wide variety of techniques at its disposal, not just a series of acts but a continuing and multiform process. There could be many kinds of representation, participation and accountability, appropriate to different circumstances and linked to particular functions. As the American democratic theorist, Robert Dahl, has put it, once it is recognized that democracy is 'an array of possibilities' then 'the prey we have been stalking is the proposition that democratic authority requires a variety of forms. The democratic idea is too grand to be trivialized by restricting itself to only one form of authority.'[5] It can be territorial and functional, mixing modes of representation and participation, a matter of many arenas and levels. Those early twentieth-century British theorists who, in assorted ways, sought to pluralize the idea of democracy and citizenship, refusing an omnicompetent and undifferentiated definition, had grasped an essential point.

Indeed, the point had acquired more force at the end of the twentieth century than at the beginning, for there were now more concentrations of power in more places and all requiring a matching development of the techniques of democracy. This was clearly true of the modern state, but it was also true of the 'private states' represented by the big corporations and financial institutions: each presented challenges to democratic governance and to conceptions of citizenship. At the same time, the developing global organization of power meant that it was necessary to build connections between traditional accounts of democracy and citizenship within the domestic arena of the nation-state and the enlarged accounts required by participation in the arena of international institutions.[6] All these are real difficulties and challenges, for all societies professing a commitment to democratic government, but they are made more intractable than they need be in Britain by those aspects of a political tradition which refuse to allow the categories by which they might be addressed. Thus an attachment to an indivisible 'sovereignty', located in lone institutional form, not only makes it difficult to come to terms with a world in which sovereignty is diffused and pluralized but makes it even more difficult – more difficult than it need be – to develop appropriate institutional responses.

Yet such responses are precisely what big government, with its 'complex interdependence'[7] of public and private, state and market, require if there is to be both effectiveness and democracy. If government in Britain lacks the requisite machinery (as it does), then this has to be seen not as an institutional oversight but as a direct expression of the kind of political traditions discussed here. The absence of secure forms of sub-central government, the lack of independent institutions that are more than the creatures of the government of the day, the failure to develop the apparatus of social and economic participation; all this, and more, properly reflects a politics of subjecthood rather than of citizenship. It is scarcely surprising, therefore, that invitations to move in a more 'European' direction have met with a cool and confused response, in a context where 'to construct a European-style social market in Britain, along German lines, requires participative economic, political and social actors that do not exist.'[8]

This also serves as a reminder that citizenship, like democracy, is not just a matter of the constitutional rules of the game (although in Britain the constitutional aspect has become pressing and inescapable), but also a matter of defining in a more general sense what membership of a political community entails in terms of both state and civil society, with that definition then given formal expression and protection. Here, too, recent argument clarifies what is at stake. The putative privatization of citizenship at the hands of the neo-liberals of the New Right has had a twin focus: it was to be both depoliticized and desocialized. Both were aspects of the same project. Any response, therefore, needed also to take up both; not just to reaffirm the public and political character of citizenship, and its constitutional dimension, but in addition to anchor 'democratic citizenship' in a solid foundation of rights and entitlements.[9] In a famous text, T. H. Marshall may have been wrong to depict a cumulative historical coalition of civil, political and social and economic citizenship,[10] but he had not been wrong to want to see it in that way. Indeed, in post-war Britain there was wide assent to the view that a citizenship settlement of this kind was what was taking place. Its fragile roots were only fully exposed when, a generation later, there began the vigorous enterprise of digging it up. When not merely political rights were attacked, but also economic and social rights, it became easier to see how they were related and why any attempt to operationalize a democratic conception of citizenship had to embrace a similarly wide front.

This was liberal in the sense that it was necessary to think in terms of the protection of individual rights against public power in face of the neo-liberal onslaught, and on the need for proper constitutional guarantees, but in other respects it was necessary to move beyond traditional liberalism. There was, firstly, the need to conjoin civil and political rights with economic and social rights, but there was also the need to respond to those who would take the politics out of citizenship by reclaiming a 'civic republican' or communitarian position in which citizens were active participants in shaping public (and not merely individual) purposes. There was much scope for lively philosophical debate here, because a democratic citizenship of this kind (combining public purpose with pluralism, political with social rights, community with diversity, liberty with equality) had to be constructed and not merely reconstructed.[11]

These issues, of course, go way beyond the British case, where they were heard only as philosophical echoes of local arguments, and touch the modern condition itself. But the local arguments matter, especially to locals. Philosophers only have to interpret the world; citizens have to live in it. And living in Britain, with all its ordered decency, has meant inhabiting a polity in which Dunning's celebrated parliamentary motion of 1780 that the 'power of the executive has increased, is increasing and ought to be diminished' continues to describe the essence of the matter, notwithstanding the intervening arrival of electoral democracy. I have sought here to identify some of the reasons for this, especially in terms of the politics of ideas in Britain, as well as some of its consequences. Likewise, I have wanted to suggest that the process of strengthening and deepening democracy in Britain needs to be seen not in terms of a quick institutional fix, even if that was possible, but as a related process of both institutional and theoretical change. There are, fortunately, some hopeful signs that this is beginning to be understood.

But matters are urgent. This is not just because the neo-liberal right has made ruthless use of the powers made available to governments by a Crown-in-Parliament constitution to engineer its shift from politics to markets, but because any response has ceased to have the option of a return to a *status quo ante* but has to forge its own version of an enabling and empowering state. The argument here is that this means a complex democracy, distinguished by a dense variety of techniques of representation, participation and accountability, embedded in a secure constitutional framework, and grounded in an articulated statement of the rights and entitlements of citizenship. Power will need to move upwards (beyond the nation-state), downwards and wider. A different kind of politics, a different way of *doing* politics, needs to be explored.[12] The corrosion of community and the privatization of social life needs accessible public arenas in which identities can be affirmed and the practice of citizenship nourished. All this is made more difficult than it need be in Britain by the sinking hull of sovereignty, beyond rescue but still able to block the way. When it finally goes down what will have been lost is a state for subjects. What could be gained is a democracy for citizens.

20

Postscript on prospects

The arena of power and influence has become narrower and bleaker since I first looked at Britain's anatomy thirty years ago . . .

Anthony Sampson *The Essential Anatomy of Britain* (1992)

But is it going to happen? Is the British *ancien régime*, rooted in its pre-democratic traditions, institutions and habits of mind, poised to make a historical transition to a modern constitutional democracy? If it is, how is such a process of change to come about – and where is its driving force to be looked for?

It has to be admitted at once that the prospects (in mid-1993) can seem very bleak indeed, even getting bleaker. With one party in power for so long, with four consecutive election victories under its belt, democracy becomes increasingly confined to the arenas of disagreement within the governing party. This is conspicuously so on the issue of Europe; but it is scarcely less so on other issues (such as the coal closure programme or the future of the welfare state). Between elections democracy becomes a matter of Conservative party management. There is ever less need to consult and negotiate beyond this circle; and ever more capacity to make the world in the image of the governing party. The appointive state at the disposal of ministerial patronage can be framed ever more tightly to fit correct political perspectives. The civil service increasingly learns that its role is not to be a disinterested reservoir of policy advice in the public interest, but rather a compliant tool of ministers. Ministers themselves freely repudiate any application of the principle of ministerial responsibility when their policies collapse, thus cancelling the traditional British bargain whereby exceptional power was balanced by an exceptional and final responsibility.

Nor is this all. Legislation can be driven through without detailed preparation, research or advice (the latest Education Bill is an outstanding example)[1] and with key elements to be filled out later by ministerial *diktat*. When ministers are caught out (for example, in promoting arms sales to Iraq when Parliament was told they were not, or in having their private legal bills paid from public funds), this is usually only by accidental leak or spillage, and the fall-out becomes only another task for political management. Independent sources of scrutiny and policy are progressively snuffed out or replaced by more domesticated instruments. An elaborate and lavish spoils system comes to distinguish the relations between the governing party and its financial donors and influential supporters. The players learn to accept the new rules of the governing game – and the penalties for breaking them. A pervasive whiff of corruption begins to fill the air.

Yet even this, which may be seen just as a ruling arrogance born of an extended tenure of office in a system with a remarkable absence of constitutional constraints, does not fully describe the developments currently taking place. For it is accompanied by an ideological redefinition of government itself, in the direction of 'business government' in which public institutions and services are increasingly put out to market on a contractual basis and run by managers who are freed up from political restraint. Indeed, almost without notice, both local government and the civil service are being revolutionized in precisely this way. This is not, it should be emphasized, merely a matter of achieving wholly desirable objectives of better managed and more efficient government, but a process whereby politics is dissolved into administration. Government, both national and local, is to be no more than a holding company. There is to be nothing distinctive about a public interest (except in so far as it can also be someone's private interest) and nothing distinctive about a public service (for that is increasingly performed by market operators whose bottom line is cost, profit and shareholders). Who needs politics anyway?

What this process means – and the prospect it implies – is not just a matter of rubbing along with a pre-democratic, top-down kind of government which happens to have been monopolized by a single party, though that would be serious enough and a sufficient agenda for constitutional reflection and reform. The additional seriousness derives from the redefinition of government itself that such a system is enabling to be put in place. This involves a privatization of citizenship and a dissolution of accountability. Political consumers are left to pursue their 'rights' and make their complaints in relation to services over which they have ever less control and ever less expectation of control, in an invisible fog of non-accountability, deprived of the means of effective collective action and of independent agencies of support and scrutiny. Truly a world in which nobody is responsible for anything anymore – a central virtue claimed for markets, but a terminal vice when transferred to politics.

All this may seem sufficient to warrant a thoroughly gloomy conclusion, especially when the divided character of the opposition forces are added in to the account. Yet there are some contra-indications too. Above all, perhaps, it is far from clear that Britain can be governed on these terms, or at least governed successfully. A range of voices (now including some from the business community) are to be heard arguing that a successful economy requires a more participative and co-operative policy process with the institutions to match. The contradiction between a doctrine of 'subsidiarity' espoused as a defence against the writ of the European Community and a rigid domestic centralism has been apparent for all to see. The failure to engage the people – and, worse, the failure to see the need to engage the people – in the Maastricht ratification process has exposed a deeper failure of democratic citizenship. It is becoming increasingly difficult for governments to exempt themselves from the freer flow of information (or at least to find convincing reasons for such exemption), and to claim that the protection of rights can safely be left to a sovereign Parliament. There is a growing recognition that parliamentary sovereignty is the constitutional name for executive rule and party domination.

Indeed, it is scarcely too much to say that the *ancien régime* is coming apart at the seams. Even the monarchy is no longer immune. The governing response may still be to fiddle with the fraying seams, stitching and adjusting here and there (a bit more official information, a little royal taxation), but this only serves to highlight the need for more thoroughgoing reform. It is not difficult to see why Britain's governing arrangements have come to be as they are; but it is difficult to see how they can continue to be as they are. The very seamlessness of constitutional matters means that one thing necessarily leads to another.[2] It may be possible to reform by instalments, perhaps through a roving commission,[3] but there is a chain of inescapable connections. This has been well understood by the defenders of the status quo, who know precisely what they are defending – and what they stand to lose once the constitutional unpicking begins.

All the signs are, though, that the fabric will not hold and that a period of constitutional politics lies ahead. Moreover, the agenda is reasonably clear, as the earlier discussion here has tried to show. The central task is to reconstitutionalize British government; and the associated task is to constitutionalize those 'private' governments where concentrated and unaccountable power also looms large. Yet, as the earlier discussion argued too, this is less a matter of a series of mechanical or institutional reforms (however far-reaching in their scope) and much more a matter of cultural and ideological change. This is the hardest kind of change, because it touches on identity and traditional ways of seeing the world. In this context, it means a shift away from an adversarial, monopolistic model of party government to a new kind of pluralism, a new way of *doing* politics.

The traditional model has found its perfect embodiment in British constitutional arrangements. For the same reason any significant alteration in those arrangements implies a new political model, in some respects a more 'European' model of negotiated and consensus-building politics. It is vigorously pluralistic, seeks to provide guarantees for institutions and individuals against easy incursion, and espouses a collaborative governing style. It is only necessary to register such features to be reminded of the extent to which they are alien to the British way of politics. But this may now, finally, be changing. It is possible to see the Labour Party's sponsorship of a Commission on Social Justice, deliberately constructed to stretch beyond party lines, as a harbinger of this different kind of politics, certainly if supplemented with further similar initiatives and combined with a concerted attempt to assemble a new progressive coalition around both constitutional and social change.

It would, though, be unwise to be excessively sanguine about this prospect. Conservatives, of both right and left, will always prefer the world of monopolitic parties and no-nonsense sovereignty. However, there will surely be many others for whom the prospect of a pluralistic, learning kind of politics will seem a more engaging project for the governing of complex societies in the public interest than the traditional model that, in Britain, is now in such conspicuous disarray. One version of democracy is probably dead, even if its successor has yet to be born.

Notes and references

1 The image and the system

1 House of Commons 30 October 1990 (*Parl. Deb.*, col. 873). In his ensuing resignation speech, Sir Geoffrey Howe argued that 'we commit a serious error if we think always in terms of "surrendering" sovereignty' (House of Commons, 13 November 1990 (*Parl. Deb.*, col. 463)).
2 H. J. Laski *A Grammar of Politics*, London: Allen & Unwin, 1925, p. 430.
3 Ibid., pp. 44–5.
4 G. Poggi *The Development of the Modern State*, London: Hutchinson, 1978, p. 141.
5 C. B. Macpherson *The Real World of Democracy*, London: Oxford University Press, 1966, p. 5.
6 P. Self *Administrative Theory and Politics*, London: Allen & Unwin, 1972, p. 292.
7 For example, D. Held *Models of Democracy*, Cambridge: Polity, 1987, for an excellent review; and D. Held and C. Pollitt *New Forms of Democracy*, London: Sage, 1986, for some interesting applications.
8 *Democracy in a World of Tensions*, UNESCO, Paris: 1951; cited in S. Benn and R. Peters *Social Principles and the Democratic State*, London: Allen & Unwin, 1959, p. 332.
9 A. L. Lowell *The Government of England*, vol. 2, London: Macmillan, 1908, p. 507.
10 A. Mathiot *The British Political System*, London: Hogarth, 1958, p. 335.
11 The key texts are S. Beer *Modern British Politics*, London: Faber, 1965; and A. H. Birch *Representative and Responsible Government*, London: Allen & Unwin, 1964. For a longer view, L. Tivey *Interpretations of British Politics*, Hemel Hempstead: Harvester, 1988, is excellent.

2 The place and the problem

1 R. McKibbin 'The franchise factor in the rise of the Labour Party' in his *The Ideologies of Class*, Oxford: Oxford University Press, 1990, pp. 67–8.
2 R. H. Tawney *Democracy or Defeat*, London: WEA, 1917.
3 R. Muir *How Britain is Governed*, London: Constable, 1930, p. 4.
4 T. H. Marshall *Citizenship and Social Class and Other Essays*, Cambridge: Cambridge University Press, 1950.
5 *Report of the Committee of Inquiry on Industrial Democracy*, Cmnd 6706, London: HMSO, 1977.
6 The species was examined in R. McKenzie and A. Silver *Angels in Marble*, London: Heinemann, 1968.
7 G. Orwell *The Road to Wigan Pier*, (1937), Harmondsworth: Penguin, 1962, p. 137.
8 J. Roper *Democracy and its Critics: Anglo-American Democratic Thought in the Nineteenth Century*, London: Unwin Hyman, 1989, p. 12.
9 Ibid., p. 211. Indeed, for an argument that what did define it was an 'authoritarian individualism', see Jonathan Clark 'The history of Britain: a composite state in a *Europe des patries?*' in J. C. D. Clark (ed.) *Ideas and Politics in Modern Britain*, London: Macmillan, 1990, pp. 32–49.
10 G. Marshall and G. Moodie *Some Problems of the Constitution*, London: Hutchinson, 1959, pp. 15–18.
11 'The idea of the State is one which is little grasped in England' announced Ernest Barker in 'The "rule of law" ', *Political Quarterly*, May 1914, p. 139. For discussion of the British case, see Rodney Barker, 'The rise and eclipse of the social democratic state' in R. Borthwick and J. Spence *British Politics in Perspective*, Leicester: Leicester University Press, 1984, pp. 1–18; and, for its oddity, K. Dyson *The State Tradition in Western Europe*, Oxford: Martin Robertson, 1980.

3 Democracy and the constitution: New wine, old bottles

1 A. V. Dicey *Introduction to the Study of the Law of the Constitution*, 10th edition, London: Macmillan, 1959, pp. 91, 128.
2 Ibid., p. 40.
3 Ibid., p. 199.
4 Ibid., p. 79.
5 Ibid., p. 84.
6 Ibid., p. 83.
7 Ibid., p. 431.
8 Ibid., p. 453.
9 Ibid., p. 468.
10 Ibid., p. 471.
11 A. V. Dicey 'The Parliament Act 1911 and the destruction of all constitutional safeguards', in his *The Rights of Citizenship*, London:

1912, pp. 91, 92. For discussion, see J. Meadowcroft and M. Taylor 'Liberalism and the referendum in British political thought 1890–1914', *Twentieth Century British History*, vol. I, no. 1, 1990, pp. 35–57.

12 A. V. Dicey 'Unionists and the House of Lords', *National Review*, 24, 1895, p. 690; and 'Ought the referendum to be introduced into England?', *Contemporary Review*, 57, 1890, p. 497.

13 M. Ostrogorski *Democracy and the Organisation of Political Parties*, 2 vols, London: Macmillan, 1902.

14 H. Morrison *Government and Parliament*, London: Oxford University Press, 1954, p. 98.

15 T. Smith 'The British constitution: unwritten and unravelled', in J. Hayward and P. Norton (eds) *The Political Science of British Politics*, Brighton: Wheatsheaf, 1986, p. 66.

4 Dominocracy

1 J. McEldowney 'Dicey in historical perspective – a review essay', in P. McAuslan and J. McEldowney (eds) *Law, Legitimacy and the Constitution*, London: Sweet and Maxwell, 1985, p. 59.

2 Michael O'Donnell ' "See that action is taken to silence Mr. Guy" – yours, the Minister', *Guardian*, 24 June 1987.

3 W. Blackstone *Commentaries on the Laws of England*, 1765–9.

4 Lord Scarman, Radcliffe Lecture, University of Warwick, May 1988, extract published in *Guardian*, 27 June 1988.

5 Debate in the House of Lords on 'The executive power of government', House of Lords, 2 March 1988 (Fifth Series, vol. 494). The whole of this short debate is illuminating and worth reading.

6 W. L. Miller *Irrelevant Elections? The Quality of Local Democracy in Britain*, Oxford: Clarendon, 1988, p. 226.

7 K. Ewing and C. Geary *Freedom Under Thatcher: Civil Liberties in Modern Britain*, Oxford: Clarendon, 1990, p. v. In another review, a leading public lawyer observed: 'The Government has a truly wonderful magic wand; it is called "The Three Line Whip". When it is waved with the incantation "Parliamentary Sovereignty", a great and mysterious and sometimes terrible thing called an Act of Parliament is brought into being which can turn right into wrong, justice into injustice and subvert the rule of law', G. Zellick, 'Government beyond law', *Public Law*, 1985, p. 288.

8 *Index on Censorship*, vol. 17, no. 8, September 1988.

9 *Attorney-General v. Guardian Newspapers Ltd (No. 2)* [1988] 3 All ER 545.

10 The whole appalling story is dissected in J. Gibson *The Politics and Economics of the Poll Tax: Mrs Thatcher's Downfall*, Cradley Heath: Emas, 1990.

11 'A scent of sleaziness pervades the air', *Observer*, editorial, 21 December 1986.

5 Doubts and discontents

1 Examples might include A. King (ed.) *Why is Britain Becoming Harder to Govern?*, London: BBC, 1976, and R. E. Tyrrell *The Future That Doesn't Work: Social Democracy's Failures in Britain*, New York: Doubleday, 1977. For discussion, see A. W. Wright 'What sort of crisis?', *Political Quarterly*, vol. 48, no. 3, 1977.

2 J. D. B. Mitchell 'Administrative law and policy effectiveness', in J. A. G. Griffith (ed.) *From Policy to Administration: Essays in Honour of W. A. Robson*, London: Allen and Unwin, 1976, p. 198; M. Partington 'The reform of public law in Britain: theoretical problems and practical considerations', in P. McAuslan and J. McEldowney (eds) *Law, Legitimacy and the Constitution*, London: Sweet and Maxwell, 1985, p. 199. The consequence was that 'the modern state crept up, in a sense unobserved, upon both politicians and lawyers' (Mitchell, ibid., p. 181).

3 This is discussed in A. W. Wright 'British decline: political or economic?', *Parliamentary Affairs*, vol. 40, 1987.

4 S. Brittan 'The economic consequences of democracy' in R. Skidelsky (ed.) *The End of the Keynesian Era*, London: Macmillan, 1977, p. 49. For an argument that older fears about the perils of 'mass democracy' were 'truly prophetic', see R. Moss *The Collapse of Democracy*, London: Temple Smith, 1975, especially Chapter 2.

5 S. Brittan 'The economic tensions of British democracy', in Tyrrell op. cit., p. 141.

6 For example, N. Johnson *In Search of the Constitution*, London: Methuen, 1980. This should now be supplemented with Ferdinand Mount *The British Constitution Now*, London: Heinemann, 1992.

7 K. Minogue in K. Minogue and M. Biddiss (eds) *Thatcherism: Personality and Politics*, London: Macmillan, 1987, p. 17. Even the *Wall Street Journal* noticed: Barbara Timan 'Tory paradox: in Thatcher's Britain, free enterprise leads to more state control', October, 1988.

8 The 1970s had already started the process. The evidence is displayed in J. Alt *The Politics of Economic Decline*, Cambridge: Cambridge University Press, 1979.

9 P. Hirst 'Extending Democracy' in his *Law, Socialism and Democracy*, 1986, p. 116.

10 In the words of one manifesto from the left in the early 1980s, 'socialists must broaden the back of government, and strengthen the rod that beats it', F. Cripps *et al. Manifesto: A Radical Strategy for Britain's Future*, London: Pan, 1981, pp. 147–8.

11 K. Middlemass *Power, Competition and the State, Vol 1: Britain in Search of Balance 1940–1961*, London: Macmillan, 1986, p. 8.

6 Representative government revisited

1 A. H. Birch *Representative and Responsible Government*, London: Allen & Unwin, 1964, p. 130.

2 James Mill *An Essay on Government* (1820), Cambridge: 1937, p. 34.
3 J. S. Mill *Considerations on Representative Government* (1861), London: Dent, 1964.
4 This point is well made in D. Oliver 'The parties and parliament: representative or intra-party democracy?' in J. Jowell and D. Oliver (eds) *The Changing Constitution*, Oxford: Clarendon, 1985, pp. 103–26.
5 On the development of a 'disorganised politics', see the discussion in S. Hall and M. Jacques *New Times*, London: Lawrence and Wishart, 1989.
6 A reminder that its 'traditional form' is less traditional than often supposed is provided by A. Beattie 'The two-party legend', *Political Quarterly*, vol. 45, 1974, pp. 288–99.
7 F. Ridley 'At the bottom of the democracy league', *Guardian*, 10 August 1987.
8 T. Paine *Rights of Man* (1791), Harmondsworth: Penguin, 1977, p. 215. For discussion see C. Harlow 'Power from the people? Representation and constitutional theory', in P. McAuslan and J. McEldowney (eds) *Law, Legitimacy and the Constitution*, London: Sweet and Maxwell, 1985, pp. 62–81.
9 As described, for example, in J. Richardson and A. Jordan *Governing under Pressure: The Policy Process in a Post-Parliamentary Democracy*, Oxford: Martin Robertson, 1979.
10 K. Ewing, 'Trade unions and the constitution: the impact of the New Conservatives', in C. Graham and T. Prosser (eds) *Waiving the Rules: The Constitution under Thatcherism*, Stony Stratford: Open University Press, 1988, p. 152.
11 J. A. Hobson *The Crisis of Liberalism*, London, 1909, p. 41.

7 Responsible government revisited

1 As endless surveys have revealed, including a vast Reader's Digest survey in 1990 of public attitudes towards institutions across Europe (reported in the *Guardian*, 12 February 1991).
2 Enoch Powell, House of Commons, 20 February 1979 (*Parl. Deb.*, col. 336); cited in C. Turpin, 'Ministerial responsibility: myth or reality?' in J. Jowell and D. Oliver (eds) *The Changing Constitution*, Oxford: Clarendon, 1985, p. 63.
3 S. E. Finer 'The individual responsibility of Ministers', *Public Administration*, vol. 34, 1956.
4 Nor, because of the infirmities of oppositions, is it reliably effective. See P. Hennessy *The Hidden Wiring*, Fabian Society Discussion Paper, 1990.
5 For example, B. Crick *The Reform of Parliament*, London: Weidenfeld, 1963.
6 First report of the Select Committee on Procedure, HC 588, 1977/8.
7 D. Oliver and R. Austin, 'Political and constitutional aspects of the Westland affair', *Parliamentary Affairs*, vol. 40, 1987.

8 George Jones 'Send the watchdogs packing', *The Times*, November 4, 1989.
9 The joke is explained in H. Heclo and A. Wildavsky *The Private Government of Public Money*, London: Macmillan, 1974.
10 M. Sunkin 'What is happening to applications for judicial review?', *Modern Law Review*, vol. 50, 1987, pp. 432–67.

8 Political culture: Democracy unvisited

1 Bryce Papers, 15 December 1901; cited in J. McEldowney 'Dicey in historical perspective – a review essay', in P. McAuslan and J. McEldowney (eds) *Law, Legitimacy and the Constitution*, London: Sweet and Maxwell, 1985, p. 61.
2 Quoted in S. Benn and R. Peters *Social Principles and the Democratic State*, London: Allen and Unwin, 1959, p. 333.
3 Introduction to W. Bagehot *The English Constitution*, London: World's Classic edition, 1928, p. xxiv. Note also, more surprisingly perhaps, Harold Laski's statement that: 'The decency of English political life, not a little, also, of its creativeness, is built on the fact that men who face one another over the benches of the House of Commons have enough social intimacy to join their minds in making a common solution of difficult problems before the breaking-point is reached.' (*A Grammar of Politics*, London: Allen & Unwin, 1925, p. 409).
4 A. Almond and S. Verba *The Civic Culture: Political Attitudes and Democracy in Five Nations*, Princeton: Princeton University Press, 1963. The taming of democracy by deference in England had been a central theme of Dicey: 'Democracy in modern England has shown a singular tolerance, not to say admiration, for the kind of social inequalities involved in the existence of the Crown and of an hereditary and titled peerage; a cynic might even suggest that the easy working of modern English constitutionalism proves how beneficial may be in practice the result of democracy tempered by snobbishness.' (*Lectures on the Relation between Law and Public Opinion in England during the Nineteenth Century*, London: Macmillan, second edition, 1914, p. 57.)
5 S. Beer *Britain Against Itself*, London: Faber, 1982.
6 D. Kavanagh 'The deferential English: a comparative critique', *Government And Opposition*, 1971, 6, pp. 333–60; A. Marsh *Protest and Political Consciousness*, London: Sage, 1977; A. Heath and R. Topf 'Political culture', in R. Jowell, S. Witherspoon and L. Brook (eds) *British Social Attidues: the 1987 Report*, Social and Community Planning Research, Aldershot: Gower, pp. 51–67.
7 V. Hart *Distrust and Democracy*, Cambridge: Cambridge University Press, 1978.
8 D. Marquand *The Unprincipled Society*, London: Cape, 1988, Chapter 7.
9 Hugo Young 'Giving a hoot, mon, for democracy', *Guardian*, 15 September 1988.

10 Patrick Nairne 'Yes Minister, please tell us more', *The Times* 8 May 1990.
11 R. H. S. Crossman 'Towards a philosophy of socialism' in Crossman (ed) *New Fabian Essays*, London: Turnstile, 1952, pp. 28–9.
12 E. C. S. Wade 'Introduction to Dicey', in his *Introduction to the Study of the Law of the Constitution*, London: Macmillan, 10th edition, 1959, p. cxcvi.
13 'Panorama', BBC, 25 January 1988.
14 R. Dworkin 'Devaluing liberty', *Index on Censorship*, vol. 17, no. 8, September 1988, p. 7.

9 Democracy and ideology: The left

1 Alastair Darling MP, quoted in A. Wright 'British socialists and the British Constitution', *Parliamentary Affairs*, vol. 43, 1990, p. 322. I draw upon this article for some of the discussion here.
2 *Report on Fabian Policy*, London: Fabian Society, 1896.
3 K. O. Morgan *Labour in Power 1945–51*, Oxford: Clarendon, 1984, pp. 84, 494. Labour's 'constitutional inhibitions' over a long period are traced in B. Jones and M. Keating *Labour and the British State*, London: Oxford University Press, 1985.
4 H. Morrison *Government and Parliament*, London: Oxford University Press, 1954, p. 92.
5 G. D. H. Cole *A Plan for Britain*, Clarion Press, 1932, p. 39.
6 J. R. MacDonald *Socialism and Government*, Vol. I, London: Independent Labour Party, 1909, p. xxviii.
7 *New Statesman*, 1 January 1955, quoted in G. Marshall and G. Moodie *Some Problems of the Constitution*, London: Hutchinson, 1959, p. 101.
8 H. J. Laski *A Grammar of Politics*, London: Allen and Unwin, 1925, pp. 348, 314.
9 'The common thrust of arguments . . . has been towards a deflation of democratic pretensions': J. Lively *Democracy*, Oxford: Blackwell, 1975, p. 5.
10 House of Commons, 8 October 1940; quoted in J. Campbell *Nye Bevan and the Mirage of British Socialism*, London: Weidenfeld and Nicolson, 1987, p. 98.
11 J. A. G. Griffith 'Justice and administrative law revisited' in J. A. G. Griffith ed. *From Policy to Administration: Essays in Honour of William A. Robson*, London: George Allen and Unwin, 1976, pp. 204–5.
12 H. R. G. Greaves *The British Constitution*, London: Allen and Unwin, 1948 (2nd edition), pp. 271–2. A more recent text from the *Marxisant* left organized around 'the "democratic" mythology' of British politics is R. Miliband *Capitalist Democracy in Britain*, Oxford: Oxford University Press, 1982.
13 *Samizdat* no. 3, 1989.
14 David Held 'The contemporary polarisation of democratic theory: the case for a third way' in his *Political Theory and the Modern State*, Cambridge: Polity, 1989, p. 182.

10 Democracry and ideology: The right

1 P. Clark *A Question of Leadership*, London: Hamish Hamilton, 1991, p. 104.
2 'Analysis', BBC Radio 4, 6 April 1989. Powell adds: 'I'm prepared to call it democracy just to keep in with the Americans.'
3 L. S. Amery *Thoughts on the Constitution*, London: Oxford University Press, 1947, p. 21.
4 Edmund Burke *An Appeal from the New to the Old Whigs* (1791).
5 'Conservatives in local government', *The Citizen*, December 1947, reproduced in *Conservatism 1945–1950*, London: Conservative Political Centre, 1950, pp. 166–8.
6 This 'dialectic' – not just within the Conservative tradition, but within British politics generally – is the theme of W. H. Greenleaf *The British Political Tradition: Volume 2, The Ideological Heritage*, London: Routledge, 1983.
7 Lord Hailsham *The Dilemma of Democracy*, London: Collins, 1978, pp. 21, 68.
8 F. A. Hayek *The Political Order of a Free People*, London: Routledge, 1979. For discussion of the new Conservative constitutionalism, see C. Graham and T. Prosser 'The constitution and the new Conservatives' in their edited volume *Waiving the Rules: The Constitution under Thatcherism*, Milton Keynes: Open University Press, 1988; also N. Johnson, 'Constitutional reform: some dilemmas for a Conservative philosophy' in Z. Layton-Henry (ed.) *Conservative Party Politics*, London: Macmillan, 1980.
9 Hailsham op. cit, pp. 9–10.
10 A. Gamble 'Economic decline and the crisis of legitimacy', in C. Graham and T. Prosser, op. cit, p. 31.
11 As any reader of R. Moss *The Collapse of Democracy* (London: Temple Smith, 1975) would have discovered.
12 On this see J. Bulpitt 'The Thatcher statecraft', *Political Studies*, 1986.

11 The missing traditions

1 S. H. Beer *Modern British Politics*, London: Faber, 1965, pp. 70, 91.
2 The best account remains A. H. Birch *Representative and Responsible Government*, London: George Allen and Unwin, 1964 (especially Chapter 5 on 'The liberal view of the constitution').
3 H. J. Laski *Reflections on the Constitution*: Manchester, Manchester University Press, 1951, p. 54.
4 S. Webb and B. Webb *A Constitution for the Socialist Commonwealth of Great Britain* (1920), Cambridge: Cambridge University Press, 1975, pp. 72–3.
5 There was constitutional Bennery, of course, but this too was rooted in a traditional attachment to the 'sovereignty of Parliament' (as in T. Benn, *Parliament, People and Power*, London: Verso, 1982).
6 This is discussed in the concluding chapter of C. Graham and T.

Prosser (eds) *Waiving the Rules: The Constitution under Thatcherism*, pp. 186–8.

7   A. H. Halsey *Change in British Society*. Oxford: Oxford Univesity Press, Second edition, 1981, p. 84.

8   Halsey, op. cit., p. 85.

9   P. McAuslan and J. McEldowney, 'Legitimacy and the constitution: the dissonance between theory and practice' in P. McAuslan and J. McEldowney (eds) *Law, Legitimacy and the Constitution*, London: Sweet and Maxwell, 1985, p. 8.

10 Adam Raphael 'Honours that carry a whiff of corruption', *Observer*, 23 December 1990.

11 Adam Raphael 'Members who lobby in their own interest', *Observer*, 16 April 1989.

12 J. Grigg, 'Making government responsible to Parliament', in R. Holme and M. Elliott, (eds) *1688–1988: Time For a New Constitution*, London: Macmillan, 1988, p. 170.

13 D. Marquand *The Progressive Dilemma*, London: Heinemann, 1991.

12 Centralism and localism

1   On federalism, Foreign Secretary Douglas Hurd professed not to understand it: 'the definitions of federalism are multiple and contradictory' and so it was 'simply not sensible to use the word' (House of Commons, 26 June 1991 (*Parl. Deb.* col. 1012)). On sovereignty, Bernard Crick has wisely remarked that: 'The concept has become not the key to British constitutional thought, but the rust in the lock' ('Sovereignty, centralism and devolution' in R. Holme and M. Elliott, (eds) *1688–1988: Time For a New Constitution*, London: Macmillan, 1988, p. 67.

2   A neat summary is provided in S. Leach and G. Stoker 'The transformation of central–local government relationships' in C. Graham and T. Prosser *Waiving the Rules: The Constitution under Thatcherism*, Milton Keynes: Open University, 1988, pp. 95–115. Also see Howard Davies 'Local government under siege', *Public Administration*, vol. 66, no. 1, Spring 1988.

3   Maud Committee Report: *Management of Local Government, vol. 1*, 1967.

4   K. Young and M. Davies *Local Government Since Widdicombe*, Joseph Rowntree Foundation, 1990; also J. Gyford, S. Leach and C. Game *The Changing Politics of Local Government*, London: Unwin Hyman, 1989.

5   For evidence and discussion see C. Crouch and D. Marquand (eds) *The New Centralism: Britain Out of Step in Europe*, Oxford: Blackwell, 1989; and Will Hutton 'Creeping paranoia threatens economy', *Guardian* 13 June 1990.

6   A. Sancton 'British socialist theory of the division of power by area', *Political Studies*, vol. 24, 1976, pp. 158–70.

7 J. Bulpitt *Territory and Power in the United Kingdom*, Manchester: Manchester University Press, 1983.

8 On this 'puzzle' see L. J. Sharpe, 'The Labour Party and the geography of inequality: a puzzle' in D. Kavanagh (ed.) *The Politics of the Labour Party*, London: George Allen and Unwin, 1982, pp. 135–70.

9 Bulpitt, op. cit., p. 130.

10 A robust examination of the issues from that period is A. H. Birch *Political Integration and Disintegration in the British Isles*, London: George Allen & Unwin, 1977. Note its concluding remark that: 'Whatever happens to the Scotland and Wales Bill, it seems clear that the United Kingdom is entering a new phase in its history, in which the centralised system of goverment that has served for the past two centuries will have to be modified' (p. 167).

11 R. A. W. Rhodes *Beyond Westminster and Whitehall: The Sub-Central Governments of Britain*, London: Allen & Unwin, 1988.

13 Consumers, producers and citizens

1 S. Webb and B. Webb *A Constitution for the Socialist Commonwealth of Great Britain* (1920), Cambridge: Cambridge University Press, 1975, pp. xxxix–xliv. On the arguments of this period, see P. Hirst (ed.) *The Pluralist Theory of the State*, London: Routledge, 1989.

2 K. Middlemass *Power, Competiton and the State Vol. 1: Britain in Search of Balance 1940–1961*, London: Macmillan, 1986.

3 D. Marquand *The Unprincipled Society*, London: Cape, 1988, p. 148.

4 On this, see I. Harden 'Corporatism without Labour: the British version' in Graham and Prosser, op. cit., pp. 36–55.

5 A theme forcefully argued in P. Hirst *After Thatcher*, London: Collins, 1989.

6 On this task see R. Plant *Citizenship, Rights and Socialism*, London: Fabian Society, 1988.

7 The proposition, and the support, is reviewed in A. W. Wright *G. D. H. Cole and Socialist Democracy*, Oxford: Clarendon, 1979.

8 R. Dahl *A Preface to Economic Democracy*, Cambridge: Polity, 1985, pp. 161–2.

9 Note, from the radical right, John Redwood's remark: 'Privatisation is not and need not be a movement of the radical right' ('Popular capitalism and world politics' in J. C. D. Clark (ed.) *Ideas and Politics in Modern Britain*, London: Macmillan, 1990, p. 222.

10 *The Citizen's Charter*, HMSO, Cm 1599, July 1991.

11 For discussion of this, see N. Deakin and A. Wright, (eds) *Consuming Public Services*, London: Routledge, 1990.

12 R. Klein 'The politics of participation', in R. Maxwell and N. Weaver (eds) *Public Participation in Health*, London: King's Fund, 1984, p. 20.

13 Klein, ibid. On this point see also J. Potter 'Consumerism and the public sector: how well does the coat fit?' in *Public Administration*, vol. 66, no. 2, 1988, pp. 149–64 (Special issue on 'Consumerism and beyond').

14 G. Mulgan, 'Power to the Public', *Marxism Today*, May 1991.

14 Reconstructions I: Representation

1 I. McLean 'Forms of representation and systems of voting', in D. Held (ed.) *Political Theory Today*, Cambridge: Polity, 1991, p. 172.
2 Ibid., pp. 173–6.
3 C. Harlow 'Power from the people? Representation and constitutional theory', in P. McAuslan and J. McEldowney, (eds) *Law, Legitimacy and the Constitution*, London: Sweet and Maxwell, 1985, p. 81.
4 P. Hirst 'Representative democracy and its limits', *Political Quarterly*, vol. 59, no. 2, 1988, p. 190.
5 G. D. H. Cole *Social Theory*, London: Methuen, 1920, p. 106.
6 Ibid., pp. 106–8.
7 On this, see the Introduction to P. Hirst (ed.) *The Pluralist Theory of the State*, London: Routledge, 1989.
8 R. Williams 'Democracy and Parliament' (1982), in R. Gable (ed.) *Resources of Hope*, London, Verso, 1989, p. 274. Writing about 'The Arts Council'(1979), Williams identified the problem of 'all-purpose representation' in relation to regional arts associations as an example of 'this endlessly displaced and deflected mode of public representation, this virtually unargued and untraceable translation of a general occasional vote into an apparent authority to decide highly specific issues' (*Resources of Hope*, p. 51).
9 *The Plant Report*, 1991 (*Guardian Studies*), with its declaration that: 'We do not believe that the same electoral system has to be followed for all representative institutions' (p. 99).
10 A notable invitation comes from J. Burnheim *Is Democracy Possible?* Cambridge: Polity, 1985.

15 Reconstructions II: Accountability

1 J. S. Mill *Considerations on Representative Government* (1861) in A. D. Lindsay (ed.) *Utilitarianism, Liberty, Representative Government*, London: Dent, 1964, p. 239. Note also Mill's other function for Parliament: 'to be at once the nation's Committee of Grievances, and its Congress of Opinions' (ibid.).
2 As described in P. Day and R. Klein *Accountabilities: Five Public Services*, London: Tavistock, 1987.
3 The adjective is Enoch Powell's, the metaphor Austin Mitchell's.
4 An example of this view is R. Wendt 'Elected bodies and appointed bodies', *Local Government Studies*, January/February 1986.
5 P. Day and R. Klein op. cit., pp. 228–9.
6 On this see *The Constitution of the United Kingdom*, Institute for Public Policy Research, 1991. The issue of entrenched legal rights has, for reformers, always been clouded by 'a little local difficulty – the peculiar history and structure of the legal profession here' (L. Lustgarten,

'Socialism and the Rule of Law', *Journal of Law and Society*, vol. 15, 1988, p. 31).

7 Even the Major Government, after the 1992 election, offered self-denial as the appropriate constitutional path, notably in relation to a range of secrecy provisions.

8 P. Hennessy *The Hidden Wiring*, Fabian Society Discussion Paper, 1990, p. 4.

9 I am thinking particularly of Bernard Crick, whose *The Reform of Parliament* (Weidenfeld & Nicholson, 1964) defined an earlier debate. His revisionism is traced in his memorial essay 'Stuart Walkland and parliamentary realism', *Political Studies*, vol. 27, 1989.

10 On this see 'The state of the nation' (1973) in E. Powell *Reflections of a Statesman: Writings and Speeches*, London: Bellew, 1991, pp. 249–53.

11 Hennessy op. cit., suggests that oppositions have been routinely ineffective as agents of accountability in the post-war period.

12 'It is time for us to think of the building of a variety of democratic institutions rather than concentrating on Parliament as *the* institutional form' (T. Prosser 'Democratisation, accountability and institutional design: reflections on public law', in P. McAuslan and J. McEldowney (eds) *Law, Legitimacy and the Constitution*, London: Sweet and Maxwell, 1985, p. 189.

13 This is the proposal to be found in I. Harden and N. Lewis *The Noble Lie: The British Constitution and the Rule of Law*, London: Hutchinson, 1986.

16 Reconstructions III: Participation

1 C. Pateman *Participation and Democratic Theory*, Cambridge: Cambridge University Press, 1970; D. Held *Models of Democracy*, Cambridge, Polity, 1987.

2 Skeffington Report: *People and Planning. Report of the Committee on Public Participation in Planning*, London: HMSO, 1969, p. 1.

3 N. Boaden *et. al. Public Participation in Local Services*, London: Longman, 1982, p. 179. A similarly gloomy verdict is delivered by P. Birkenshaw *Grievances, Remedies and the State*, London: Sweet and Maxwell, 1985. A useful source for the period is A. Barker *Public Participation in Britain: A Classified Bibliography*, London: Bedford Square Press, 1979.

4 R. Klein 'The politics of participation' in R. Maxwell and N. Weaver (eds) *Public Participation in Health*, London: King's Fund, 1984, p. 25. A point developed, from a different perspective, by A. Phillips, *Engendering Democracy*, Cambridge: Polity, 1991.

5 On this see *Preparing for Partnership: Governor Training Evaluation for the City of Birmingham*, Birmingham: School of Education, University of Birmingham, 1991.

6 The volume and variety of participation in Britain is charted in G. Parry *et al. Political Participation and Democracy in Britain*, Cambridge University Press, 1992.

7 The theme of I. Harden and N. Lewis *The Noble Lie: The British Constitution and the Rule of Law*, London: Hutchinson, 1986.

8 G. D. H. Cole *Essays in Social Theory*, London: 1950, p. 102.

9 There is an interesting discussion of the democratic possibilities of advisory councils chosen by lot in R. Dahl *After the Revolution?*, New Haven and London: Yale, 1970, pp. 149–53; while H. Laski *A Grammar of Politics*, London, Allen and Unwin, 1925, ch. 8 passim, also advocated an advisory network as the basis for citizenship. User councils for public services are proposed by N. Deakin and A. Wright *Consuming Public Services*, London: Routledge, 1990, p. 211.

10 S. Webb and B. Webb *A Constitution for the Socialist Commonwealth of Great Britain*, 1920, pp. 224 ff. On this also see the evidence and argument of W. Hampton *Democracy and Community*, London: Oxford University Press, 1970.

11 R. Hambleton 'Consumerism, decentralisation and local democracy', *Public Administration* vol. 66, no. 2, 1988, 125–47.

12 V. Bogdanor *The People and the Party System: The Referendum and Electoral Reform in British Politics*, Cambridge: Cambridge University Press, 1981.

13 I. McLean 'Mechanisms for democracy', in D. Held and C. Pollitt (eds) *New Forms of Democracy*, London: Sage, 1986, pp. 135–57.

14 B. Crick 'Participation and the future of government', in J. A. G. Griffith (ed.) *From Policy to Administration*, London: Allen & Unwin, 1976, p. 62.

17 Reconstruction IV: Openness

1 P. Nairne, 'Yes Minister, please tell us more', *The Times* 8 May 1990.

2 Lord Hailsham *The Dilemma of Democracy*, London: Collins, 1978, p. 157. Note the converging verdicts of Lord Hailsham ('the real government machine, its operative parts, its personnel, its committees, its agenda, its conclusions, its ethos, its traditions, is shrouded in mystery, its deliberations secretively concealed behind the legal fiction', ibid., p. 155) and Tony Benn ('the democracy of which we boast is becoming a decorous facade behind which those who have power exercise it for their own advantage and to the detriment of the public welfare', *Arguments for Democracy*, London: Cape, 1981, p. 4).

3 *R. v Ponting* [1985] and C. Ponting *The Right to Know*, London: Sphere, 1985, pp. 190–1.

4 The existence of the cabinet committee system was finally revealed to an astonished public in mid-1992, along with the cabinet handbook *Questions of Procedure for Ministers*.

5 See 'How the cards are stacked', *Guardian*, 15 March 1989, for a detailed inventory.

6 For examples see 'Democracy in Britain retarded by secrecy', *Independent*, 22 July 1991; and for commentary, B. Levin, 'Even about the dead they lie', *The Times*, 1 August 1991. The best account of routine

secrecy remains R. Delbridge and M. Smith (eds) *Consuming Secrets*, London: Burnett, 1982.

7 J. Cornford, 'Official secrecy and freedom of information', in R. Holme and M. Elliott (eds) *1688–1988: Time For a New Constitution*, London: Macmillan, 1988, p. 145.

8 This point is well made in R. Austin, 'Freedom of information: the constitutional impact', in J. Jowell and D. Oliver (eds) *The Changing Constitution*, Oxford: Clarendon, second edition, 1989, which I have found very helpful for this section.

9 Including the replacement of Polaris by Trident as the British deterrent system. On this, and other issues, see J. Greenaway, S. Smith and J. Street, *Deciding Factors in British Politics*, London: Routledge, 1992.

10 The minister responsible for implementing the charter, William Waldegrave, has done a trawl through Whitehall looking for areas where the veil of secrecy might safely be lifted. Welcome though this is, it still represents the traditional approach at work, with the executive deciding what information to release and what to withhold, designed – like previous such initiatives – to head off demands for more fundamental reform to secure open government.

11 The *locus classicus* here may be seen as Tony Benn's diary record (*Conflicts of Interests: 1977–1981*) of the deliberations of the Callaghan Government ('Thursday 15 March, 1979 – we came to open government, and Jim said he found the subject unutterably boring . . .' etc.).

12 Austin, op. cit., p.446. For a draft bill, the basis for private members' legislation, see *A Freedom of Information Act for Britain*, Campaign for Freedom of Information, 1991.

13 D. Ashford *Policy and Politics in Britain*, Oxford: Blackwell, 1981, p. 16.

18 The end of politics?

1 J. C. D. Clark 'The history of Britain: a composite state in a *Europe des Patries*?' in J. C. D. Clark (ed.) *Ideas and Politics in Modern Britain*, London: Macmillan, 1990, p. 41.

2 One of the best discussions of sources and applications is N. Bosanquet *After the New Right*, Aldershot: Dartmouth, 1989. On the strategy of depoliticization, M. Pirie *Micropolitics*, London: Wildwood, 1988 is instructive.

3 Z. Bauman, 'Britain's exit from politics', *New Statesman and Society* 29 July 1988. On this consumerist politics of 'exit', in place of a collective politics of 'voice', A. Hirschman *Exit, Voice and Loyalty*, Cambridge: Mass., Harvard University Press, 1970, in indispensable.

4 This step is effectively taken in the *Consultation Paper on the Future Structure of Local Government*, Department of the Environment, 1991.

5 A. J. Polin *Lenin and the End of Politics*, London: Methuen, 1984.

6 S. Brittan *Participation without Politics*, London: Institute of Economic Affairs, 1975.

7 Hugo Young, 'Why Tories sing the future belongs to me', *Guardian*, 15 November, 1988.
8 On this resolution – with the conclusion that 'it is time once more for the "governing of men" to take precedence over "the administration of things" if a democratic politics is to be sustained in Britain' – see T. Smith 'The British Constitution: unwritten and unravelled' in J. Hayward and P. Norton (eds), *The Political Science of British Politics*, Brighton: Wheatsheaf, 1986, pp. 65–84.
9 S. Ranson, 'From 1944 to 1988: education, citizenship and democracy', *Local Government Studies*, vol 14, 1988. pp. 1–19. The process may be seen as reaching its apotheosis with the White Paper *Choice and Diversity: A New Framework for Schools* (London: HMSO, Cm 2021, July 1992) presaging the formal dismemberment of the postwar education system.
10 P. Hirst, 'Associational socialism in a pluralist state', *Journal of Law and Society*, vol. 15, 1988, p. 140.

19 Becoming citizens

1 D. Heater *Citizenship: The Civic Ideal in World History, Politics and Education*, London: Longman, 1990, provides a useful guide.
2 J. Patten 'Launching the active citizen', *Guardian*, 28 September 1988; D. Hurd 'Freedom will flourish where citizens accept responsibility', *Independent*, 13 September 1989.
3 N. Ascherson 'Citizens put on the active list', *Observer*, 16 October 1988. See also D. Marquand 'Subversive language of citizenship', *Guardian*, 2 January 1989.
4 R. Barker *Political Legitimacy and the State*, Oxford: Clarendon, 1990, p. 3.
5 R. Dahl *After the Revolution?* New Haven and London, Yale University Press, 1970, pp. 59, 67. On this, see also P. Hirst 'Extending democracy' in his *Law, Socialism and Democracy*, London: Allen & Unwin, 1986, pp. 108–23.
6 D. Held, 'Democracy, the nation-state and the global system', in D. Held (ed.) *Political Theory Today*, Cambridge: Polity, 1991, pp. 197–235.
7 J. Cornford *et al*; *Next Left: An Agenda for the 1990s*, Institute for Public Policy Research, 1992.
8 Will Hutton 'Britain's strange kind of democracy', *Guardian* 28 October 1991.
9 R. Plant *Citizenship, Rights and Socialism*, London: Fabian Society, 1988. For discussion, see the interview with Sir Ralf Dahrendorf, 'Decade of the citizen', *Guardian*, 1 August 1990.
10 T. H. Marshall *Citizenship and Social Class and Other Essays*, Cambridge: Cambridge University Press, 1950.
11 The philosophical terrain is neatly surveyed and discussed by Chantal Mouffe, 'The civics lesson', *New Statesman and Society*, 7 October 1988, pp. 28–31.

12 For a seductive prospect of 'politics as mutual education' see the final
   chapter of David Marquand *The Unprincipled Society*, London: Cape,
   1988. See also Richard Crossman's similar plea in 1945 in Britain's
   'closed' political culture, quoted in A. Howard, *Crossman*, London:
   Cape, 1990, p. 9.

20 Postscript on prospects

1 This Bill was preceded by an appropriately shoddy White Paper, as
   Stuart Maclure (among many others) observed: 'Is it my imagination
   or is this White Paper not unbelievably bad? Bad in the sense of poor
   quality – far below the standard you expect from a great department
   of state? Could you imagine David Eccles, Edward Boyle or Anthony
   Crosland – or for that matter, Margaret Thatcher or Keith Joseph –
   putting out such a slipshod and windy White Paper? And here is John
   Patten proudly boasting he wrote the first and worst chapter himself.
   O tempora, O mores'. 'Buy my pig in a poke.' *Times Educational Supplement*, 4 September 1992.
2 James Cornford 'Towards a Constitutional Equation?', in B. Crick
   (ed.) *National Identities: The Constitution of the United Kingdom*, Oxford:
   Blackwell, 1991, pp. 157–67.
3 As suggested, for example, by R. Brazier, *Constitutional Reform*,
   Oxford: Clarendon, 1991.

Index